Are You Thinking What I'm Thinking?

Are You Thinking What I'm Thinking?

500 Fascinating Opinion Polls and Attraction Survey

Sam Westbrook

iUniverse, Inc.
New York Lincoln Shanghai

Are You Thinking What I'm Thinking?
500 Fascinating Opinion Polls and Attraction Survey

iUniverse, Inc.

For information address:
iUniverse, Inc.
2021 Pine Lake Road, Suite 100
Lincoln, NE 68512
www.iuniverse.com

The polls contained in this book are non-scientific and reflect only the views of those who chose to participate. They should be used for entertainment purposes only.

ISBN: 0-595-32797-4

Printed in the United States of America

Contents

Introduction

Each of us has a natural human curiosity about the world in which we live and about those with whom we interact. We want to know if others share our views. We want to know if our neighbors make the same mistakes and have the same habits we do. We want to know what others think but don't dare say. Often, these curiosities go unanswered, except perhaps by those with whom we closely associate. *Are You Thinking What I'm Thinking?* helps to reveal the mind of the public and answer some of the intriguing questions that confront us each day.

About the Book

Are You Thinking What I'm Thinking? contains a compilation of polls conducted on the internet over the span of nearly two years. These polls gauge public opinion on matters ranging from the war on terror, to kissing on the first date. The questions were inspired by a variety means—books, news, television, and people, to name a few. In short, they were inspired by what we experience in our every day lives.

To gather responses, polls were placed on a website open to the general internet public. Visitors were allowed to select one answer and vote only one time for each opinion poll. Web log statistics reveal that most of the respondents were from the United States; however, many other countries were represented in the responses, including: England, Scotland, Wales, Australia, and Canada.

How to Use This Book

Are You Thinking What I'm Thinking? was created to provide you with fun and though-provoking entertainment. This book can really be used anytime or anywhere, but here are a few suggestions for when it may come in handy:

- When you need an idea to kick-start a conversation
- When you need some inspiration for a paper or talk
- When you want to take an introspective look at your opinions and how they compare to others

- When you want ask your friends and family how they feel about a certain topic

Are You Thinking What I'm Thinking? can always give you something to think or talk about. Use it when needed as a great cure for boredom!

Code Guide

Throughout the book, codes will appear next to various polls in order to give you an idea as to the type of question the poll presents. Here is a guide to the codes you will see:

- ☑ COM—Complaints
- ☑ CON—Controversial
- ☑ CUR—Current Events
- ☑ FAV—Favorites
- ☑ FUT—Future
- ☑ HYP—Hypothetical

Business

☒ **Do you read through contracts before you sign them?**

Yes, always

[▭] 21.4%

Yes, most of the time

[▭] 44.9%

Sometimes

[▭] 21.4%

No, not usually

[▭] 11.2%

No, never

[▭] 1.0%

Responses: 98

☒ **Which auto brand has the worst looking vehicles?**

Land Rover

[▭] 22.4%

Geo

[▭] 20.4%

Hyundai

[▭] 14.3%

Kia

[▭] 10.2%

Volkswagen

[▭] 9.2%

Suzuki

[▭] 7.1%

Saturn

[▭] 4.1%

None of the above

[▭] 12.2%

Responses: 98

☒ **Does Microsoft use unethical business practices in keeping and gaining market share?**

Yes
[████] 29.5%
No
[█████] 41.1%
I'm not sure
[████] 29.5%

Responses: 129

☒ **Should corporate executives take a pay cut before laying off employees?**

Yes
[████████████] 88.0%
No
[□] 7.2%
I'm not sure
[□] 4.8%

Responses: 125

☒ **What do you think about insurance premiums that are based on age and sex?**

It's sound business practice
[█████] 48.3%
It's discrimination
[████] 40.3%
I'm not sure
[□] 11.4%

Responses: 149

☒ **What is to blame for the rising price of health insurance?**

Lawsuit-happy citizens
[████] 43.6%
Insurance companies
[███] 35.1%

Jury awards

☐   14.9%

Doctors

☐   6.4%

Responses: 94

☒If there were a national movement to abandon Microsoft software, would you participate?

Yes

☐   9.5%   ☑HYP

No

☐ 80.0%

I'm not sure

☐   10.5%

Responses: 95

☒Have you ever thought about starting your own business?

Yes

☐ 66.0%

No

☐   22.9%

I already have my own business

☐   11.1%

Responses: 144

☒What type of shipping do you normally choose when you order something?

Standard ground (1 –2 weeks)

☐ 82.7%

Express (2–3 days)

☐   15.4%

Overnight

☐ 1.9%

Responses: 104

Driving

☒ How fast do you drive on average?

Slower than the speed limit
☐ 1.4%

About the speed limit
▭ 11.1%

1 to 5 mph above the limit
▭ 38.2%

5 to 10 mph above the limit
▭ 39.6%

More than 10 mph above the limit
☐ 9.7%

Responses: 144

☒ What is the most distracting driving behavior?

Talking on the cell phone
▭ 40.3%

Attending to children
▭ 26.8%

Putting on makeup
▭ 24.2%

Eating
☐ 6.0%

Talking to passengers
☐ 2.0%

Adjusting the radio
☐ 0.7%

Responses: 149

☒ How would you rate your driving skills?

Greatly above average

☐ 25.7%

Moderately above average

☐ 45.6%

Average

☐ 25.7%

Moderately below average

☐ 1.5%

Greatly below average

☐ 1.5%

Responses: 136

☒ What do you consider a safe amount of speed to travel over the speed limit without getting a ticket?

1–2 mph

☐ 3.8%

3–4 mph

☐ 15.0%

5–6 mph

☐ 49.6%

7–8 mph

☐ 12.0%

9–10 mph

☐ 17.3%

Over 10 mph

☐ 2.3%

Responses: 133

☒ If you arrived at a stoplight that just turned red and there was no visible traffic, would you run the light?

Yes

☐ 3.6%

Yes, only if I was in a hurry

☐ 8.4%

☑ HYP

No

☐ 86.7%

I'm not sure

☐ 1.2%

Responses: 83

☒Why do semi-trucks bother you?

I can't see anything when I'm behind one

☐ 28.4%

They act like they own the road

☐ 25.9%

They take up too much room

☐ 8.6%

They drive too slow

☐ 3.7%

Semi-trucks don't bother me

☐ 33.3%

Responses: 81

☑COM

☒When you are driving, how often do you find yourself getting very angry at other drivers?

At least once a day

☐ 24.4%

A couple times a week

☐ 6.4%

About once a week

☐ 15.4%

A couple times a month

☐ 12.8%

A few times a year

☐ 21.8%

Almost never

☐ 15.4%

Never

☐ 3.8%

Responses: 78

☒How would you vote on a proposition that would remove speed limits on the freeways?

Yes, remove speed limits

☑HYP

20.7%

No, don't remove speed limits

69.4%

I'm not sure

9.9%

Responses: 121

☒How long do you think it will be until flying cars are the norm?

Less than 20 years

☑FUT

2.9%

20–40 years

17.1%

40–60 years

15.7%

60–80 years

5.7%

More than 80 years

24.3%

Flying cars will never become the norm

34.3%

Responses: 70

☒Have you ever received a speeding ticket?

Yes

63.5%

No

36.5%

Responses: 115

☒Have you ever been in an automobile accident?

Yes, a minor accident

58.3%

Yes, a major accident

☐ 23.6%

Never

☐ 18.1%

Responses: 72

☒How would you vote on a proposition that would ban using cell phones while driving?

Yes, ban using cell phones while driving

☐ 46.2%   ☑HYP

No, don't ban using cell phones while driving

☐ 42.5%

I'm not sure

☐ 11.3%

Responses: 106

☒Have you ever stopped to help a stranded motorist?

Yes

☐ 52.6%

No

☐ 47.4%

Responses: 78

☒What point would the price of gasoline have to reach for you to consider cutting back on driving?

-Poll Date: 28-Sep-2003

It's already there

☐ 36.6%

$2.00/gallon

☐ 14.1%

$2.50/gallon

☐ 16.9%

$3.00/gallon

☐ 12.7%

$3.50/gallon

☐ 4.2%

More than $3.50/gallon

☐ 15.5%

Responses: 71

☒Are you more of a fast lane driver or a slow lane driver?

Fast lane

☐ 68.2%

Slow lane

☐ 31.8%

Responses: 107

☒What do you consider the rudest driving behavior?

Cutting people off

☐ 42.5%   ☑COM

Tailgating

☐ 27.6%

Not using a turn signal

☐ 16.1%

Talking on a cell phone

☐ 13.8%

Responses: 87

☒Which country makes the best automobiles?

United States

☐ 37.0%

Japan

☐ 33.7%

Germany

☐ 28.3%

Other

☐ 1.1%

Responses: 92

☒What sports car would you most like to have?

Lamborghini

☐ 21.1%

Porsche
☐ 21.1%

Viper
☐ 12.3%

Ferrari
☐ 12.3%

Corvette
☐ 10.5%

Lotus
☐ 1.8%

Other
☐ 21.1%

Responses: 57

☒When was the last time you ran a red light?

Within the past week
☐ 14.3%

Within the past month
☐ 15.7%

Within the past year
☐ 14.3%

More than a year ago
☐ 28.6%

I've never run a red light
☐ 27.1%

Responses: 70

Entertainment

⊠ What is your favorite type of music?

Rock

☑ **FAV**

33.3%

Country

14.7%

Pop

14.7%

Rap

10.7%

Classical

10.7%

Other

16.0%

Responses: 75

⊠ What is your favorite theme park?

Disneyworld

☑ **FAV**

27.7%

Six Flags

23.1%

Disneyland

21.5%

Sea World

9.2%

Universal Studios

6.2%

Busch Gardens

3.1%

MGM Studios

1.5%

Other
☐   7.7%
Responses: 65

☒ Would the world be a better place if there were no T.V.?

Yes
☐   28.4%

No
☐   60.8%

I'm not sure
☐   10.8%

Responses: 74

☑ **HYP**

☒ How do you feel about restrictions on network television content?

They should be more stringent
☐   40.6%

They are fine how they are
☐   37.7%

They should be loosened
☐   21.7%

Responses: 106

☑ **CON**

☒ When you watch Jeopardy, you think…

This is boring
☐   14.8%

Hey, I should be up there
☐   34.1%

Wow, those people are smart
☐   25.9%

I wish Alex Trebek would stop trying to be witty
☐   25.2%

Responses: 135

☒ How do you feel about copying CDs/DVDs?

It's ok for personal use
☐   50.5%

I'm indifferent

☐ 17.2%

I don't see a problem with it

☐ 12.9%

Serves them right for charging so much

☐ 9.7%

It's not ok under any circumstances

☐ 6.5%

Those companies make too much money anyway

☐ 3.2%

Responses: 93

☒What is your favorite way to watch a movie?

At home with a DVD/video cassette rental

☐ 42.9%   ☑**FAV**

Go to the theater

☐ 41.6%

At home on regular T.V.

☐ 15.6%

Responses: 77

☒What type of movie do you most like to watch?

Comedy

☐ 43.6%   ☑**FAV**

Action/Adventure

☐ 28.2%

Drama

☐ 16.4%

Horror

☐ 8.2%

Romance

☐ 3.6%

Responses: 110

☒Which one of these major T.V. networks do you like most?
-Poll Date: 10-Feb-2003

FOX

☑FAV

| | 38.0% |

NBC

| | 34.7% |

CBS

| | 16.5% |

ABC

| | 10.7% |

Responses: 121

☒What T.V. reality show would you most like to be on?
-Poll Date: 21-Feb-2003

Survivor

☑HYP

| | 13.2% |

Real World

| | 6.6% |

The Bachelor/Bachelorette

| | 6.6% |

Are You Hot?

| | 2.9% |

American Idol

| | 2.2% |

I would never want to be on a reality T.V. show

| | 62.5% |

Other

| | 5.9% |

Responses: 136

☒Would you want to ride the tallest and fastest roller coaster in the world?

You bet!

☑HYP

| | 51.1% |

No way!

| | 48.9%

Responses: 141

☒Who is your favorite character from the T.V. show Friends?
-Poll Date: 14-Apr-2003

Joey

| | 15.7%   ☑**FAV**

Chandler

| | 12.1%

Phoebe

| | 10.7%

Rachel

| | 9.3%

Monica

| 4.3%

Ross

| 3.6%

I don't watch Friends

| | 44.3%

Responses: 140

☒Will computer animated films be able to match the realism of human actors?
-Poll Date: 18-Apr-2003

Yes

| | 42.6%   ☑**FUT**

No

| | 45.4%

I'm not sure

| | 12.0%

Responses: 108

☒If you were offered the chance to be on a reality T.V. show, would you take it?

Yes

| | 20.9%   ☑**HYP**

No

63.4%

I'm not sure

15.7%

Responses: 134

☒Which games do you like most?

Card games   ☑**FAV**

33.6%

Video games

25.0%

Outdoor games

21.6%

Board games

19.8%

Responses: 116

☒Who did you want to win American Idol?

-Poll Date: 18-Jun-2003

Clay Aiken   ☑**CUR**

19.0%

Ruben Studdard

25.4%

What American Idol?

55.6%

Responses: 126

☒What best describes your feelings about movie critics?

I don't read movie reviews

27.1%

What makes their opinion so important??

24.0%

I find their opinions to be interesting/helpful

21.9%

They're usually wrong

11.5%

How did they ever become a move critic??

☐   10.4%

They're usually right

☐   5.2%

Responses: 96

☒What do you most like to watch on T.V.?

Sitcoms

☐ 19.6%   ☑**FAV**

Movies

☐ 16.7%

Documentaries

☐ 16.7%

Reality shows

☐ 13.7%

Dramas

☐ 10.8%

Sports events

☐ 8.8%

News

☐ 7.8%

Other

☐ 5.9%

Responses: 102

☒You have a King and a Five (value of 15) in a game of Blackjack. What do you do?

Hit

☐ 57.5%   ☑**HYP**

Stand

☐ 26.4%

Split

☐ 3.8%

Surrender

☐ 0.9%

I don't know how to play Blackjack

☐   11.3%

Responses: 106

☒ Which would you pick in a game of Truth or Dare?

Truth

☑ **HYP**

79.7%

Dare

20.3%

Responses: 74

☒ Who is your favorite late night talk show host?

David Letterman

☑ **FAV**

35.7%

Jay Leno

27.1%

Conan O'Brien

12.9%

Jimmy Kimmel

2.9%

None of the above

21.4%

Responses: 70

☒ How would you cope without a T.V.?

I couldn't survive

☑ **HYP**

10.5%

It would be difficult but I would get used to it

49.1%

It wouldn't be so bad

24.6%

No T.V.? No problem

15.8%

Responses: 114

☒ What sci-fi series do you like best, Star Wars or Star Trek?

Star Wars

☑ FAV

☐ 41.7%

Star Trek

☐ 20.4%

I like them both about the same

☐ 13.0%

I don't like either of them

☐ 25.0%

Responses: 108

☒ Who would win in a duel between Batman and Spiderman?

Spiderman

☑ HYP

☐ 51.1%

Batman

☐ 48.9%

Responses: 88

☒ How many of the ads on T.V. do you believe are deceptive in some way?

All of them

☐ 16.0%

Most

☐ 48.0%

About half

☐ 24.0%

Few

☐ 12.0%

None

☐ 0.0%

Responses: 75

☒ What are the ratings of the movies you usually watch?

Un-rated

☐ 2.9%

R

44.3%

PG-13

40.0%

PG

4.3%

G

4.3%

Other

4.3%

Responses: 70

☒Which is your favorite Star Wars movie?
-Poll Date: 19-Dec-2003

Episode I: The Phantom Menace

15.2%

Episode II: Attack of the Clones

6.1%

Episode IV: A New Hope

19.7%

Episode V: The Empire Strikes Back

33.3%

Episode VI: Return of the Jedi

25.8%

Responses: 66

☑**FAV**

☒Which T.V. program would you rather watch?
-Poll Date: 31-Dec-2003

NFL Game

31.3%

CSI

23.8%

Friends

21.3%

Survivor

13.8%

The West Wing

☐   7.5%

NBA Game

☐   2.5%

Responses: 80

☒Should censorship of network television be stricter?

Yes

☑**CON**

50.4%

No, It should stay about the same

34.5%

No, It should be less strict

15.0%

Responses: 113

☒Would you like to be the child of a famous movie star?

No

☑**HYP**

49.5%

I'm not sure

25.8%

Yes

24.7%

Responses: 97

☒What type of television content should be reduced the most?

Violent

38.8%

Sexual

26.9%

Drug

☐   9.0%

Language

☐   4.5%

None of the above

20.9%

Responses: 67

Ethics

☒ **How do you feel about cloning?**

It should be banned

| | 46.6%

☑ **CON**

It should be limited to animals only

| | 22.3%

I'm indifferent

| | 16.2%

It should be embraced

| | 14.9%

Responses: 148

☒ **If your employer made a pay increase error in your favor, would you tell them?**

Yes

| | 58.9%

☑ **HYP**

No

| | 26.6%

I'm not sure

| | 14.6%

Responses: 158

☒ **If you found $20 laying on the floor while walking through the mall, what would you do with it?**

Keep it

| | 90.9%

☑ **HYP**

Turn it over to the nearest store

☐ 5.6%

Leave it there

☐ 3.5%

Responses: 143

☒Is gambling a bad thing?

Yes

35.8%

No

56.8%

I'm not sure

7.4%

Responses: 81

☒When is it okay to lie?

Never

33.9%

Only when telling the truth would do more harm

64.2%

It's always okay

1.8%

Responses: 109

☒Is being gay morally wrong?

Yes

42.7%

No

49.5%

I'm not sure

7.8%

Responses: 103

☑CON

☒Is sex before marriage immoral?

Yes

32.2%

No

60.2%

I'm not sure

7.6%

Responses: 118

☑CON

☒Are people generally good natured or bad natured?

Good natured

[bar] 56.0%

Bad natured

[bar] 11.0%

Neither, they are in between

[bar] 29.0%

I'm not sure

[bar] 4.0%

Responses: 100

☒What is the direction of the moral state of America?

Rapidly declining

[bar] 40.3%

Slowly getting worse

[bar] 31.2%

The same as it has always been

[bar] 23.4%

Slowly improving

[bar] 5.2%

Rapidly improving

[bar] 0.0%

Responses: 77

☒What is the root of all evil?

Satan

[bar] 40.0%

Money

[bar] 36.4%

Lack of education

[bar] 18.2%

Lawyers

[bar] 3.6%

Poverty

[bar] 1.8%

Responses: 55

☒**Should gay couples be allowed to adopt children?**

Yes

☑**CON**

47.8%

No

42.6%

I'm not sure

9.6%

Responses: 115

☒**Would you rather be attractive and immoral or unattractive and moral?**

Unattractive and moral

☑**HYP**

67.6%

Attractive and immoral

32.4%

Responses: 71

☒**Is euthanasia acceptable for humans?**

Yes

☑**CON**

21.9%

Maybe in some cases

50.0%

No

28.1%

Responses: 96

☒**Is it unethical to choose the gender of your child?**

Yes

54.9%

No

29.7%

I'm not sure

15.4%

Responses: 91

Family

☒ Who handles the finances in your household?

Mother/Wife

[bar] 55.2%

Father/Husband

[bar] 33.6%

Someone else

[bar] 11.2%

Responses: 134

☒ How do you feel about spanking children as a form of discipline?

It's appropriate

[bar] 70.8%   ☑ CON

It's not appropriate

[bar] 22.9%

I'm not sure

[bar] 6.3%

Responses: 96

☒ How often does your family hold a family reunion?

More than once a year

[bar] 5.7%

Once a year

[bar] 22.9%

Once every two years

[bar] 2.9%

Once every three to five years

[bar] 11.4%

Less than once every five years

[bar] 57.1%

Responses: 70

☒ **Which one of your parents has the worst temper?**

Mom
⬜ 25.9%
Dad
⬜ 51.8%
Both are about the same
⬜ 22.4%
Responses: 85

☒ **How much should parents contribute to their children's college education?**

They should pay for all of it
⬜ 23.6%
They should pay for part of it
⬜ 54.5%
They should chip-in a little
⬜ 11.4%
The child should have to pay
⬜ 3.3%
I'm not sure
⬜ 7.3%
Responses: 123

☒ **Who or what has the greatest influence on children?**

Parents
⬜ 79.3%
Friends
⬜ 12.6%
Television
⬜ 8.1%
Religious leaders
⬜ 0.0%
Teachers
⬜ 0.0%
Responses: 111

☒Which parent is the strictest in your family?

Mom

44.9%

Dad

29.2%

They're both about the same

25.8%

Responses: 89

☒How many siblings do you have?

I'm an only child

6.3%

1–2

58.0%

3–4

24.1%

5–6

4.5%

7–8

5.4%

More than 8

1.8%

Responses: 112

☒Do you have a picture of a family member in your wallet/purse/organizer?

Yes

54.8%

No

45.2%

Responses: 104

☒Should polygamy be legalized?

I'm male and I say yes

20.0%

☑CON

I'm male and I say no

| | 80.0% |

Male Responses: 45

I'm female and I say yes

☐ 4.4%

I'm female and I say no

| | 95.6% |

Female Responses: 45

Food

☒How would you vote on a proposition that would ban alcoholic drinks?

Yes (Ban alcoholic drinks)

☑HYP

[■]   16.7%

No (Don't ban alcoholic drinks)

[■■■■■]   78.8%

I'm not sure

[■]   4.5%

Responses: 156

☒Which one of these snacks would you most like to eat?

Chips and salsa

☑FAV

[■■]   26.3%

Chocolate candy bar

[■]   19.2%

German chocolate cake

[■]   15.4%

Cheese and crackers

[■]   14.7%

Vanilla ice cream

[■]   14.1%

Tapioca pudding

[■]   5.8%

Gummy bears

[■]   4.5%

Responses: 156

☒Which cola product do you prefer?

Coca Cola

[■■]   40.3%

Pepsi

| | 36.8%

Neither

| | 10.4%

Both are good

| | 12.5%

Responses: 144

⊠What is your favorite kind of cookie?

Chocolate Chip

| | 43.4%   ☑**FAV**

Oatmeal Raisin

| | 15.8%

White Chocolate Macadamia

| | 10.5%

Peanut Butter

| | 9.2%

Oatmeal Chocolate Chip

| | 6.6%

Sugar

| | 6.6%

Ginger Bread

| | 2.0%

Other

| | 5.9%

Responses: 152

⊠What type of food do you like to eat most when you go to a restaurant?

Seafood

| | 24.3%   ☑**FAV**

Steak

| | 21.5%

Italian

| | 15.0%

Mexican
☐   14.0%
Chinese
☐   12.1%
Fast Food
☐   9.3%
Other
☐   3.7%
Responses: 107

☒ Do you have an emergency food storage?

Yes
☐   21.1%
No
☐   78.9%
Responses: 147

☒ What is your favorite type of pizza?

Pepperoni and Cheese
☐   34.0%   ☑ **FAV**
Supreme
☐   22.0%
Sausage
☐   8.0%
Cheese only
☐   7.3%
Canadian Bacon and Pineapple
☐   7.3%
Other
☐   21.3%
Responses: 150

☒ What is the most American food?

Hamburger
☐   46.1%

Hot Dog

☐ 20.3%

Fried Chicken

☐ 13.3%

Pizza

☐ 10.9%

Steak and Potatoes

☐ 8.6%

Other

☐ 0.8%

Responses: 128

☒ How do you like your eggs cooked?

Scrambled

☐ 39.1%

Over easy

☐ 37.6%

Hard-boiled

☐ 6.0%

Poached

☐ 5.3%

Other

☐ 12.0%

Responses: 133

☒ How spicy do you like your salsa?

Mild

☐ 22.6%

Medium

☐ 39.0%

Hot

☐ 28.1%

I don't like salsa

☐ 10.3%

Responses: 146

☒What is your favorite food group?

Meats/Beans
[▭]   27.7%

Sweets/Fats
[▭]   25.0%

Dairy
[▭]   16.1%

Fruits
[▭]   13.4%

Grains
[▭]   11.6%

Vegetables
[▭]   6.3%

Responses: 112

☑**FAV**

☒Which topping on a supreme pizza would you most want to take off?

Olives
[▭]   23.2%

Mushrooms
[▭]   14.6%

Onions
[▭]   13.2%

Peppers
[▭]   11.9%

Sausage
[▭]   8.6%

Pepperoni
[▭]   4.6%

I wouldn't take off any topping
[▭]   21.9%

I don't even like pizza
[▭]   2.0%

Responses: 151

☒What do you like to drink with your dinner?

Water

[====] 31.6%

Soda pop

[====] 24.8%

Milk

[===] 17.3%

Juice

[=] 6.0%

Beer

[=] 4.5%

Other

[===] 15.8%

Responses: 133

☒What type of candy chips do you like best?

Chocolate

[==========] 64.6%　　　　　　　　☑**FAV**

Butterscotch

[==] 10.1%

White Chocolate

[==] 10.1%

Peanut Butter

[==] 8.9%

I don't like candy chips

[=] 5.1%

Other

[=] 1.3%

Responses: 79

☒What canned soup do you like best?

Chicken Noodle

[===] 23.5%　　　　　　　　☑**FAV**

Clam Chowder

[==] 16.5%

Tomato
☐   15.3%
Beef Stew
☐   10.6%
Minestrone
☐   8.2%
Bean and Bacon
☐   7.1%
Broccoli and Cheese
☐   4.7%
Other
☐   14.1%

Responses: 85

☒ How much coffee do you drink?

I don't drink coffee
☐   45.7%
1 cup a day
☐   14.7%
2 cups a day
☐   14.7%
3 cups a day
☐   9.5%
4 cups a day
☐   6.0%
More than 4 cups a day
☐   9.5%

Responses: 116

☒ What is your favorite Mexican food?

Burritos
☐   21.0%   ☑ **FAV**
Tacos
☐   18.1%

Enchiladas
☐ 15.2%

Fajitas
☐ 14.3%

Nachos
☐ 12.4%

I don't like Mexican food
☐ 11.4%

Other
☐ 7.6%

Responses: 105

☒How much blame should be placed on the food industry for obesity problems?

All
☐ 0.0%

Most
☐ 2.7%

Part
☐ 27.4%

A little
☐ 21.2%

None
☐ 48.7%

Responses: 113

☑CON

☑COM

☒Which of the three traditional shake flavors do you like most?

Chocolate
☐ 48.5%

Vanilla
☐ 28.8%

Strawberry
☐ 19.7%

No preference
☐ 3.0%

Responses: 66

☑FAV

☒ What is your favorite dairy product?

Cheese

☑ **FAV**

▭▭▭▭▭	54.4%

Milk

▭▭	20.2%

Butter

▯	7.0%

Yogurt

▯	6.1%

Sour cream

▯	4.4%

I don't like dairy products

▯	1.8%

Other

▯	6.1%

Responses: 114

☒ Would you rather eat M&Ms or Skittles?

M&Ms

▭▭▭▭▭▭▭	78.8%

Skittles

▭▭	17.3%

Neither

▯	3.8%

Responses: 104

☒ What is your favorite berry?

Strawberry

☑ **FAV**

▭▭▭	42.9%

Raspberry

▭▭	23.2%

Blackberry

▭	13.4%

Blueberry

▭	13.4%

Cranberry

☐   2.7%

None of the above

☐   4.5%

Responses: 112

☒ Would you rather have a sweet pickle or a dill pickle?

Dill pickle

☐ 55.8%

Sweet pickle

☐ 18.2%

Neither/I don't like pickles

☐ 26.0%

Responses: 77

☒ How do you like your steak?

Well done

☐ 17.1%

Medium well

☐ 23.8%

Medium

☐ 21.0%

Medium rare

☐ 26.7%

Rare

☐ 6.7%

I don't eat meat

☐ 4.8%

Responses: 105

☒ How often do you go out to eat?

Almost every day

☐ 9.6%

Frequently

☐ 39.1%

Every now and then

| | 40.0%

Almost never

| | 11.3%

Never

| | 0.0%

Responses: 115

☒What is your favorite soft drink?

Pepsi

| | 27.3%   ☑**FAV**

Coke

| | 27.3%

Dr. Pepper

| | 11.7%

Cream Soda

| | 7.8%

Mountain Dew

| | 7.8%

Root Beer

| | 6.5%

Sprite

| | 5.2%

Other

| | 6.5%

Responses: 77

☒What is the best cut of meat?

Filet Mignon

| | 65.6%   ☑**FAV**

Prime Rib

| | 23.4%

Top Sirloin

| | 6.3%

Other

☐ 4.7%

Responses: 64

☒ How would you describe your breakfast?

Large sit-down breakfast

☐ 2.3%

Small sit-down breakfast

[▭] 50.0%

Small breakfast on the go

[▭] 23.3%

I don't eat breakfast

[▭] 24.4%

Responses: 86

☒ Would you rather eat Twinkies or Zingers?

Twinkies

[▭] 44.0%

Zingers

[▭] 16.0%

Neither

[▭] 40.0%

Responses: 25

☒ How full do you normally get after eating dinner?

Stuffed!

☐ 7.6%

Comfortably full

[▭] 59.8%

Just about full

[▭] 23.9%

Just full enough to get rid of the hunger

☐ 7.6%

Not full at all

☐ 1.1%

Responses: 92

☒What is your favorite kind of pancake syrup?

Maple

⬜━━━━━━━━━━━━━━⬜ 76.7%   ☑**FAV**

Blueberry

◻️ 9.6%

Boysenberry

◻️ 4.1%

Strawberry

◻️ 2.7%

Huckleberry

◻️ 1.4%

Other

◻️ 5.5%

Responses: 73

Government and Politics

☒Would Al Gore win the presidential election if he ran in 2004?
-Poll Date: 04-Oct-2002

Yes
☑CUR
18.0%

No
☑HYP
73.0%

I'm not sure
9.0%

Responses: 100

☒Should Democrats be allowed to add a new candidate for the New Jersey Senate race?
-Poll Date: 05-Oct-2002

Yes
☑CUR
37.7%

No
62.3%

Responses: 53

☒Is the Bush Administration to blame for current economic conditions?
-Poll Date: 06-Oct-2002

Yes, they haven't done enough to keep the economy going
☑CUR
34.8%

No, the economic cycle caught them in a recession
62.1%

I'm not sure
3.0%

Responses: 66

☒Are you going to vote today?
-Poll Date: 05-Nov-2002

Yes

☑CUR

55.3%

No

40.4%

I'm not old enough to vote

☐ 4.3%

Responses: 47

☒What issue should be the U.S. Government's primary focus?
-Poll Date: 18-Nov-2002

The economy

☑CUR

46.5%

Domestic terrorism

28.7%

War against Iraq

☐ 10.9%

Rebuilding Afghanistan

☐ 5.0%

Corporate scandals

☐ 4.0%

Other

☐ 5.0%

Responses: 101

☒Would you support granting amnesty to illegal aliens in the U.S.?
-Poll Date: 03-Dec-2002

Yes

☑CUR

☐ 11.9%

No

☑CON

67.9%

I'm not sure

20.1%

Responses: 134

☒Should Republican Majority Leader Trent Lott resign from his leadership position?
-Poll Date: 18-Dec-2002

Yes
☑CUR

[bar] 36.7%

No

[bar] 36.7%

I'm not sure

[bar] 26.7%

Responses: 120

☒What country is the greatest threat to the United States?
-Poll Date: 28-Dec-2002

North Korea
☑CUR

[bar] 41.0%

Iraq

[bar] 33.7%

Pakistan

[bar] 2.4%

Iran

[bar] 1.2%

Other

[bar] 21.7%

Responses: 83

☒If Hillary Clinton were to run for president in 2004, would you vote for her?
-Poll Date: 31-Dec-2002

Yes
☑HYP

[bar] 25.2%

No

[bar] 67.2%

I'm not sure

[bar] 7.6%

Responses: 119

☒What economic plan do you prefer?
-Poll Date: 08-Jan-2003

The Democrats' version
☐ 19.5%

The Republicans' version
☐ 28.8%

Neither/Undecided
☐ 24.6%

What economic plan?
☐ 27.1%

Responses: 118

☑CUR

☒How do you approve of the job President Bush is doing?
-Poll Date: 12-Jan-2003

Greatly approve
☐ 29.2%

Moderately approve
☐ 22.2%

Neutral
☐ 16.4%

Moderately disapprove
☐ 13.3%

Greatly disapprove
☐ 18.8%

Responses: 1386

☑CUR

☒Should American troops leave the Korean demilitarized zone?
-Poll Date: 23-Jan-2003

Yes
☐ 35.7%

No
☐ 50.0%

I'm not sure
☐ 14.3%

Responses: 70

☑CUR

☒ **If you had to increase/incorporate a tax, which would it be?**

Cigarette

☑ **HYP**

47.4%

Alcohol

26.3%

Sales

7.7%

Income

3.8%

Property

2.6%

Gasoline

1.9%

Other

10.3%

Responses: 156

☒ **Should the U.S. decrease its military budget and add money to other areas?**

-Poll Date: 26-Jan-2003

Yes

38.0%

No

58.2%

I'm not sure

3.8%

Responses: 79

☒ **What is the ideal type of government?**

Democracy

71.7%

Theocracy

9.1%

Socialism

7.1%

Monarchy

☐   0.0%

Other

[☐]   12.1%

Responses: 99

☒What is your opinion of the French President, Jacques Chirac?

-Poll Date: 19-Feb-2003

Highly Favorable

☐   3.7%   ☑CUR

Moderately Favorable

[☐]   9.3%

I'm indifferent

[☐☐☐☐]   41.7%

Moderately Unfavorable

[☐☐]   15.7%

Highly Unfavorable

[☐☐☐]   29.6%

Responses: 108

☒Would the world be better-off if the U.S. military withdrew from foreign lands?

-Poll Date: 25-Feb-2003

Yes

[☐☐]   22.6%

No

[☐☐☐☐]   57.5%

I'm not sure

[☐☐]   19.9%

Responses: 146

☒Is the act of protesting by facing away from the flag during the National Anthem ok?

-Poll Date: 27-Feb-2003

Yes, it is supported by the right to free speech

[☐☐]   31.3%   ☑CUR

Yes, because the government is going the wrong direction

☐   3.0%

No, it's unpatriotic

▢   12.7%

No, it's appalling and disrespectful

▭   46.3%

I'm not sure

☐   6.7%

Responses: 134

☑ CON

☒ How important is it that the U.S. ends its dependence on foreign oil?

-Poll Date: 07-Mar-2003

Extremely important

▭   33.1%

Very important

▭   37.1%

Fairly important

▭   21.0%

Not very important

☐   6.5%

Not important at all

☐   2.4%

Responses: 124

☒ Are you in favor of the Bush Administration's tax cut?

-Poll Date: 23-May-2003

Yes

▭   37.9%

No

▭   35.0%

I'm not sure

▭   27.2%

Responses: 103

☑ CUR

☒ How would you rate the government's management of your tax dollars?
-Poll Date: 01-Jun-2003

Excellent
☐   1.4%
Good
☐   7.1%
Fair
▭   41.4%
Poor
▭   50.0%
Responses: 70

☒ Do you think George W. Bush will win the presidential election in 2004?
-Poll Date: 23-Jun-2003

Yes
▭   54.6%   ☑ FUT
No
▭   28.7%
I'm not sure
▭   16.7%
Responses: 108

☒ What 1st Amendment right is most important to you?

Freedom of religion
▭   12.7%
Freedom of speech/press
▭   13.6%
Right to peaceably assemble/protest
☐   0.0%
They are all equally important
▭   71.8%
I'm not sure
☐   1.8%
Responses: 110

☒Would you vote for Arnold Schwarzenegger for governor?
-Poll Date: 08-Aug-2003

Yes
| 47.2%

No
| 28.1%

I'm not sure
| 24.7%

Responses: 89

☑CUR

☑HYP

☒Overall, do you think the impact of immigrant workers in the U.S. is positive or negative?
-Poll Date: 01-Sep-2003

Positive
| 33.3%

Negative
| 46.7%

I'm not sure
| 20.0%

Responses: 75

☒Are you in favor of the federal 'do not call' list?
-Poll Date: 25-Sep-2003

Yes
| 92.8%

No
| 2.7%

I'm not sure
| 4.5%

Responses: 111

☑CUR

☒If you could become the President of the United States, would you want to?

Yes
| 24.3%

☑HYP

No
| | 69.2%

I'm not sure
| | 6.5%

Responses: 107

☒Should senators have the power to increase their own wages?

Yes
| | 9.3%

No
| | 90.7%

I'm not sure
| | 0.0%

Responses: 107

☒What is your political alignment?

Liberal
| | 9.9%

Somewhat liberal
| | 17.6%

Moderate
| | 33.0%

Somewhat conservative
| | 20.9%

Conservative
| | 18.7%

Responses: 91

☒Should the government regulate offensive internet content?

Yes
| | 35.4%   ☑CON

No
| | 64.6%

Responses: 96

☒Do media sources carry political biases?

Yes

89.6%

No

1.0%

I'm not sure

9.4%

Responses: 96

☒Should the phrase "In God We Trust" be removed from U.S. currency?

Yes

10.3%

☑CON

No

83.8%

I'm not sure

5.9%

Responses: 68

☒Who would you vote to be president, John Kerry or George Bush?

-Poll Date: 10-Feb-2004

John Kerry

33.3%

☑CUR

George Bush

44.8%

I'm not sure

18.1%

Other

3.8%

Responses: 105

☒Should those who were born outside the U.S. be allowed to run for president?

Yes

24.3%

No

☐ 66.0%

I'm not sure

☐ 9.7%

Responses: 103

☒ Should the government be allowed to place restrictions on the amount of children a couple can have?

Yes

☐ 12.8%

No

☐ 63.8%

Maybe in overly populated countries

☐ 21.3%

I'm not sure

☐ 2.1%

Responses: 47

Health

☒Which disability would be the worst to have?

Inability to move
☐▬▬▬▬▬▬ 62.6%
Inability to see
☐▬▬ 26.1%
Inability to hear
☐ 6.1%
Inability to speak
☐ 5.2%

Responses: 115

☒How do you feel about doctor assisted suicide?

The individual should be free to decide
☐▬▬▬ 41.5%   ☑CON
It's acceptable under certain circumstances
☐▬ 27.5%
It should be illegal
☐▬ 25.4%
I'm indifferent
☐ 5.6%

Responses: 142

☒Do you smoke?

Yes
☐▬ 19.2%
No, I never have
☐▬▬▬ 55.0%
No, but I used to
☐▬ 25.8%

Responses: 151

☒ How would you like your doctor to be dressed?

In casual clothes
▢ 4.5%
In professional clothes
[▭] 38.8%
Either way is fine
[▭] 56.7%

Responses: 134

☒ Are you a healthy eater?

Very much so
▢ 7.1%
Moderately so
[▭] 33.9%
Somewhat
[▭] 33.9%
Not really
[▭] 22.3%
Not at all
▢ 2.7%

Responses: 112

☒ Which ailment would be worse: spinal meningitis or Alzheimer's?

Spinal Meningitis
[▭] 26.8%
Alzheimer's
[▭] 57.7%
I'm not sure
[▭] 15.5%

Responses: 71

☒ How bad are your allergies?

Severe
▢ 4.3%

Moderate

35.7%

Mild

31.4%

I don't have allergies

28.6%

Responses: 70

☒ Do you take a daily vitamin?

Yes

43.1%

No

56.9%

Responses: 65

☒ Are you taking prescription medicine?

Yes

54.2%

No

45.8%

Responses: 72

Holidays

☒ What is the best symbol of Halloween?

Pumpkin

[bar] 71.2%

Trick-Or-Treaters

[bar] 10.6%

Witch

[bar] 10.6%

Black Cat

[bar] 6.1%

Candy

[bar] 1.5%

Responses: 66

☒ How much do you plan to spend on Christmas shopping this year?

-Poll Date: 01-Nov-2002

Much less than last year

[bar] 21.1%

A little less than last year

[bar] 15.8%

About the same as last year

[bar] 44.7%

A little more than last year

[bar] 14.5%

A lot more than last year

[bar] 3.9%

Responses: 76

☒**What do you like most about Thanksgiving?**

Food

52.8%

Family

40.4%

Football

6.7%

Responses: 89

☒**Do you have your Christmas decorations up yet?**

-Poll Date: 09-Dec-2002

Yes

57.1%

No

30.1%

I don't celebrate Christmas

3.8%

I don't have any Christmas decorations

9.0%

Responses: 133

☒**Are you traveling for the Christmas holiday?**

-Poll Date: 22-Dec-2002

Yes

25.6%

No

74.4%

Responses: 90

☒**What is your favorite style of Christmas music?**

☑**FAV**

Popular

37.3%

Choral/Symphony

37.3%

Country

5.9%

New-Age
☐ 2.5%
Other
☐ 16.9%

Responses: 118

☒Did Santa bring you what you wanted?
-Poll Date: 25-Dec-2002

Santa was right on
☐ 27.4%
For the most part, yes
☐ 22.6%
More or less, yes
☐ 16.1%
Not really
☐ 16.1%
Not at all
☐ 17.7%

Responses: 62

☒How are you with New Year's resolutions?

I always keep them
☐ 2.3%
I usually keep them
☐ 5.7%
Sometimes I keep them
☐ 14.9%
I seldom keep them
☐ 10.3%
I never follow through
☐ 5.7%
I don't make New Year's resolutions
☐ 60.9%

Responses: 87

☒What is the best Valentine's gift?

Flowers

☐ 29.2%

Chocolates

☐ 18.3%

Intimate apparel

☐ 14.2%

Valentine's card

☐ 10.8%

Stuffed animal

☐ 4.2%

Other

☐ 23.3%

Responses: 120

☒Do you get Memorial Day off from work?

Yes

☐ 64.3%

No

☐ 35.7%

Responses: 84

☒Are you lighting fireworks at home or going somewhere else to watch?

-Poll Date: 04-Jul-2003

I'm lighting them at home

☐ 9.7%

I'm going somewhere to watch

☐ 19.4%

Both

☐ 8.1%

Neither

☐ 62.9%

Responses: 62

☒What is your favorite holiday?

Christmas

☑**FAV**

| | 59.2%

Thanksgiving

| | 14.6%

Easter

☐ 5.8%

New Year's Eve

☐ 2.9%

Independence Day

☐ 2.9%

Valentine's Day

☐ 1.9%

Other

| | 12.6%

Responses: 103

☒Is Friday the 13th really a day of bad luck?

No, it's just a myth

| | 90.9%

Yes, I've seen it

☐ 9.1%

Responses: 110

☒Do you have an artificial tree or a real tree?

Artificial

| | 55.7%

Real

| | 26.6%

I don't have a tree

| | 17.7%

Responses: 79

☒What do you think about giving your ex a Valentine's Day gift?

No way!

☐☐☐☐☐☐☐☐☐☐ 60.6%

I don't think I would do it

☐☐☐ 22.3%

I might do it

☐☐ 11.7%

Hey, that's a good idea!

☐ 5.3%

Responses: 94

Indiscretions

☒ Have you ever cheated on a test?

Yes

[bar] 74.3%

No

[bar] 25.7%

Responses: 101

☒ Have you ever parked in a handicapped parking spot?

Yes, but I was handicapped

[bar] 11.4%

Yes, I wasn't handicapped

[bar] 17.1%

No

[bar] 71.4%

Responses: 105

☒ How often do you use profanity?

All the time

[bar] 7.8%

Frequently

[bar] 21.4%

Sometimes

[bar] 26.2%

Every now and then

[bar] 17.5%

Seldom

[bar] 9.7%

Very rarely

[bar] 13.6%

Never

☐ 3.9%

Responses: 103

☒ Have you ever called into work sick when you weren't really sick?

Yes

[========================] 57.7%

No

[===============] 36.6%

Umm, I can't remember

☐ 5.6%

Responses: 71

☒ Have you ever stolen something?

Yes, something significant

☐ 10.5%

Yes, something small/insignificant

[=========================] 60.0%

Possibly, I don't remember

☐ 10.5%

No

[=======] 18.9%

Responses: 95

☒ Have you ever tried an illegal drug?

Yes

[====================] 57.3%

No

[============] 42.7%

Responses: 103

☒ Have you ever drunk alcohol as a minor?

Yes

[==================================] 87.1%

No

☐ 12.9%

Responses: 101

☒ Have you ever spent time in jail?

Yes

☐ 11.7%

No

☐────────────────☐ 88.3%

Responses: 111

☒ Have you ever cheated on your significant other?

I'm male—Yes

☐──────☐ 33.3%

I'm male—No

☐──────────☐ 66.7%

Male Responses: 51

I'm female—Yes

☐────☐ 24.1%

I'm female—No

☐───────────☐ 75.9%

Female Responses: 54

☒ What is the worst criminal offense you have committed?

Felony

☐ 3.8%

Misdemeanor

☐───☐ 16.3%

Infraction (e.g. speeding)

☐────────☐ 51.2%

None of the above

☐────☐ 28.7%

Responses: 80

☒ **Have you ever fallen asleep on the job?**

Yes

46.7%

No

53.3%

Responses: 90

Justice and the Law

☒**Are people that plead not guilty usually guilty?**

Most of the time, yes

| | 37.2%

Sometimes, yes

| | 56.5%

Most of the time, no

☐ 6.4%

Responses: 802

☒**What is your stance on capital punishment?**

For

| | 64.7%   ☑**CON**

Against

| | 23.5%

I'm not sure

☐ 11.8%

Responses: 85

☒**Should marijuana be legalized?**

Yes

| | 51.0%

No

| | 36.6%

I'm not sure

☐ 12.4%

Responses: 145

☒**Should the loser in a lawsuit pay the winner's legal expenses?**

Yes

| | 55.1%

No

32.0%

I'm not sure

12.9%

Responses: 147

☒Are current jail sentences too harsh for non-violent crimes?

Yes

38.3%

No

47.4%

I'm not sure

14.3%

Responses: 133

☒Who is most to blame for repeat criminal offenders?

The convicts themselves

85.0%

The prison system

15.0%

Responses: 120

☒Should criminal penalties be reduced for non-violent crimes?

Yes

51.7%

No

39.8%

I'm not sure

8.5%

Responses: 118

☒Would we be better off if all firearms were outlawed for citizens?

Yes

26.7%

No

62.4%

I'm not sure

10.9%

Responses: 101

Life

☒What game would you most like to play?

Monopoly
[bar] 28.7%

☑**FAV**

Poker
[bar] 21.8%

Uno
[bar] 15.8%

Pictionary
[bar] 13.9%

Chess
[bar] 8.9%

Clue
[bar] 5.9%

Charades
[bar] 5.0%

Responses: 101

☒What do you do when a telemarketer calls?

Politely tell them you're not interested
[bar] 48.3%

Abruptly hang up
[bar] 27.6%

Don't answer
[bar] 12.1%

Listen to their offer
[bar] 8.6%

Yell at them before hanging up
[bar] 3.4%

Responses: 58

☒ What is most likely to happen in the next 40 years?

Cure for cancer found

☑ **FUT**

[====] 47.7%

Humanoid intelligent robots created

[==] 20.0%

Armageddon

[=] 13.0%

Collapse of the American government

[=] 10.8%

Cold fusion invented

[] 6.7%

World peace

[] 1.8%

Responses: 818

☒ What do you do when your alarm goes off in the morning?

Get straight out of bed

[===] 30.7%

Hit the snooze button a few times before getting up

[===] 29.5%

I wake up in the morning without an alarm

[==] 22.7%

Hit the snooze button once before getting up

[=] 14.8%

Turn off the alarm and go back to sleep

[] 2.3%

Responses: 88

☒ What is the best winter activity?

Sun tanning in Arizona

☑ **FAV**

[===] 28.9%

Skiing

[==] 19.5%

Snowmobiling

[==] 15.6%

Skating

☐ 11.7%

Snowboarding

☐ 9.4%

Mountain climbing

☐ 0.8%

Other

☐ 14.1%

Responses: 128

☒ How many hours of sleep do you get per night?

5 hours or less

☐ 8.4%

5 to 6 hours

☐ 23.4%

6 to 7 hours

☐ 30.8%

7 to 8 hours

☐ 27.1%

8 to 9 hours

☐ 8.4%

9 hours or more

☐ 1.9%

Responses: 107

☒ Where would you want your children to grow up?

Small town

☐ 34.0%

Big city

☐ 5.7%

Somewhere in between

☐ 60.3%

Responses: 141

☒What is the worst chore?

Cleaning the toilet
☐ 28.7%
Mowing the lawn
☐ 21.3%
Dusting
☐ 14.8%
Washing the dishes
☐ 13.0%
Sweeping/Mopping
☐ 9.3%
Vacuuming
☐ 7.4%
Washing the laundry
☐ 5.6%
Taking out the trash
☐ 0.0%

Responses: 108

☒What is the most annoying distraction during a movie?

People talking
☐ 49.5%   ☑COM
Baby crying
☐ 31.9%
Cell phone ringing
☐ 9.9%
People walking in front of you
☐ 7.7%
Eating/opening candy
☐ 1.1%

Responses: 91

☒If you were given free hotel stay, tickets to Cairo, and you had to leave within a week, would you take the offer?

-Poll Date: 31-Mar-2003

Yes
☑HYP

☐ 33.6%

No

☐ 61.5%

I'm not sure
☐ 4.9%

Responses: 143

☒How is your luck when checking out at the store?

It seems like I always pick the slow line
☐ 27.9%

Sometimes I get in the fast lane, sometimes I don't
☐ 61.0%

I usually pick the fast lane
☐ 11.0%

Responses: 136

☒Are you bothered by people who leave their shopping carts in the parking lot instead of returning them?

Yes, greatly
☑COM

☐ 21.8%

Yes, a little
☐ 40.2%

I'm indifferent
☐ 18.4%

No
☐ 10.3%

Hey, I don't return my shopping cart
☐ 9.2%

Responses: 87

☒Would you rather host a party or go to a party?

Host a party/get-together
□ 6.2%

Go to a party/get-together
44.4%

I would like to do both about the same
17.3%

Neither
32.1%

Responses: 81

☒How many years would you like to live?

Less than 60 years
□ 1.7%

60 to 69
□ 5.0%

70 to 79
13.3%

80 to 89
33.3%

90 to 99
25.8%

100 or more years
20.8%

Responses: 120

☒Which unsolicited annoyance do you hate the most?

Telemarketer calls
43.3%

Pop-up internet ads
42.5%

Spam e-mail
□ 9.7%

Credit card applications in the mail
□ 3.0%

☑COM

Ads in the mail

☐   1.5%

Flyers at your doorstep

☐   0.0%

Responses: 134

☒After using the restroom, what do you normally do?

Rinse hands with soap and water

☐   64.1%

Rinse hands with water

☐   22.7%

Leave without washing hands

☐   13.3%

Responses: 128

☒What's your biggest neighbor pet-peeve?

Your neighbor makes too much noise

☐   16.7%   ☑COM

Your neighbor's dog barks at night

☐   13.3%

Your neighbor's house/lawn is unkempt

☐   10.0%

Your neighbor's animal _____s on your lawn

☐   6.7%

My neighbors don't do anything that bothers me

☐   36.7%

Other

☐   16.7%

Responses: 90

☒What outside temperature range do you like best?

Below 60 degrees

☐   3.3%   ☑FAV

60 to 69 degrees

☐   17.8%

70 to 79 degrees

☐ 53.3%

80 to 89 degrees

☐ 25.6%

90 degrees or warmer

☐ 0.0%

Responses: 90

☒How much do you end up spending on a vacation compared to what you planned?

Less than I planned

☐ 8.8%

The amount I planned

☐ 26.5%

More than I planned

☐ 39.2%

I don't set an amount

☐ 25.5%

Responses: 102

☒Which area would you most like to live in?

Rural

☐ 65.0%

Urban

☐ 35.0%

Responses: 120

☒Would you ever get a personalized license plate?

Yes

☐ 43.8%

No

☐ 23.8%

I used to have one

☐ 10.0%

I have one now

☐ 6.3%

I'm not sure

☐ 16.3%

Responses: 80

☒ Have you ever had a broken bone?

Yes

☐ 45.6%

No

☐ 54.4%

Responses: 103

☒ Will the general standard of living improve or decline in the next 10 years?

-Poll Date: 07-Jul-2003

Improve

☐ 32.0%

Stay about the same

☐ 38.8%

Decline

☐ 26.2%

I'm not sure

☐ 2.9%

Responses: 103

☑ **FUT**

☒ What statement do you agree with more?

Youth is wasted on the young

☐ 27.3%

Retirement is wasted on the old

☐ 9.1%

I don't agree with either statement

☐ 58.4%

I'm not sure

☐ 5.2%

Responses: 77

☒ **Have you ever purchased something from an infomercial?**

Yes
| | 37.7%
No
| | 62.3%

Responses: 69

☒ **What is most likely to happen in the next 10 years?**
-Poll Date: 28-Jul-2003

Gay marriage will be legalized in the United States
| | 31.4%   ☑**FUT**
A woman will become the President of the United States
| | 20.6%
A human will be cloned
| | 17.6%
The United States will go to war with North Korea
| | 15.7%
None of the above will happen in the next 10 years
| | 14.7%

Responses: 102

☒ **Which would be the worst to live without: running water or electricity?**

Running water
| | 59.6%
Electricity
| | 37.4%
I'm not sure
| | 3.0%

Responses: 99

☒ **Is it appropriate to include a list of where you are registered in a wedding announcement?**

Yes
| | 48.5%

No
| | 42.4%

I'm not sure
| | 9.1%

Responses: 66

☒What do you do when you are a dinner guest but don't like a food that is being served?

Avoid taking the food without mentioning it to the host
| | 44.7%

Eat the food regardless of whether you like it or not
| | 30.1%

Politely decline to eat the food
| | 14.6%

Make an excuse for why you can't eat the food
| | 4.9%

Try to make it disappear (napkin or nearby pet)
| | 3.9%

Other
| | 1.9%

Responses: 103

☒If you had to choose between living in extreme cold or extreme heat, which would you pick?

Extreme heat
| | 51.9%   ☑HYP

Extreme cold
| | 48.1%

Responses: 106

☒Have you ever locked your keys in your car?

Yes
| | 77.8%

No
| | 22.2%

Responses: 108

☒ Have you ever experienced a hurricane?

Yes

[bar] 40.7%

No

[bar] 59.3%

Responses: 108

☒ How do you feel about Mondays?

Mondays are great

[bar] 10.5%

They're okay

[bar] 27.6%

They're the same as any other business day

[bar] 30.5%

I don't care much for Mondays

[bar] 20.0%

Monday is the worst day of the week

[bar] 11.4%

Responses: 105

☒ Do you still live in your home town?

Yes

[bar] 31.7%

No

[bar] 64.4%

I don't really have a home town

[bar] 3.8%

Responses: 104

☒ At what age are children accountable for their actions?

At birth

[bar] 0.0%

2 years

[bar] 4.8%

4 years

☐   15.2%

6 years

☐   20.0%

8 years

☐   24.8%

10 years

☐   8.6%

12 years or older

☐   26.7%

Responses: 105

☒ If you were in a vegetative state, would you want to be taken off life support?

Yes

☐   75.6%   ☑ HYP

No

☐   4.2%

I'm not sure

☐   20.2%

Responses: 119

☒ Where would you like to go on a vacation?

Europe

☐   32.7%

Hawaii

☐   25.7%

Disney World

☐   8.0%

Las Vegas

☐   5.3%

New York City

☐   5.3%

Elsewhere

☐   23.0%

Responses: 113

☒What do you think is most likely to happen in the next 20 years?
-Poll Date: 03-Nov-2003

☑**FUT**

Cure for AIDS is discovered
[▭]   45.7%

Man lands on Mars
[▭]   30.2%

Armageddon
[▭]   15.5%

We have flying cars
[▯]   6.9%

World peace
[▯]   1.7%

Responses: 116

☒What daring activity would you most like to try?

Sky diving
[▭]   36.0%

Drag racing
[▭]   18.9%

Bungee jumping
[▯]   3.6%

Cliff diving
[▯]   1.8%

None of the above!
[▭]   39.6%

Responses: 111

☒What natural disaster do you fear most?

Earthquake
[▭]   37.3%

Hurricane
[▭]   20.3%

Forest fire
[▭]   15.3%

Flood

☐ 11.9%

Volcano eruption

☐ 8.5%

Tsunami

☐ 6.8%

Responses: 59

☒What is the most important factor in choosing a grocery store?

Price

☐ 38.1%

Location

☐ 25.4%

Cleanliness

☐ 23.8%

Customer service

☐ 12.7%

Responses: 63

☒What aspect of life is most important to you?

Family

☐ 70.6%

Religion

☐ 19.1%

Career

☐ 7.4%

Possessions

☐ 2.9%

Responses: 68

☒Rate how difficult your life has been.

1-Very difficult

☐ 2.0%

2

☐ 11.1%

3
☐   17.2%
4-Somewhat difficult
☐☐☐   29.3%
5
☐☐   24.2%
6
☐   14.1%
7-Cushy
☐   2.0%

Responses: 99

☒Are you trying to keep up with the Joneses?

Yes
☐   2.9%
No
☐☐☐☐☐   87.3%
We are "the Joneses"
☐☐   9.8%

Responses: 102

Money

☒ **What would you do if a homeless person asked you for money today?**

Give him some spare change

☐ 24.0%

Ignore him

☐ 22.6%

Tell him you don't have anything

☐ 19.9%

Offer to buy him some food instead of giving him money

☐ 19.0%

Depends on what they look like

☐ 8.1%

Give him a generous amount

☐ 3.6%

Tell him to get a job

☐ 2.7%

Responses: 221

☑ **HYP**

☒ **Does money bring happiness?**

Absolutely

☐ 12.6%

To some degree, yes

☐ 56.3%

Yes, but only temporarily

☐ 19.4%

Definitely not

☐ 11.7%

Responses: 103

☒What do you think about spending money on the lottery?

It's worth it, I could win
| | 34.6%

It's a waste of money
| | 47.1%

I'm not sure
| | 18.3%

Responses: 104

☒When someone wins a multi-million dollar jackpot, what do you attribute it to?

Chance
| | 48.8%

Luck
| | 43.0%

Fate
| | 8.3%

Responses: 121

☒Which one would you would rather have:

$1000 Check, Today
| | 49.0%

$2000 Check, Next Year
| | 51.0%

☑HYP

Responses: 143

☒If you won a million dollars in the lottery, would you immediately quit your job?

Yes
| | 36.7%

No
| | 51.3%

I'm not sure
| | 12.0%

☑HYP

Responses: 150

☒ **How much money would you require to wade for two minutes in Piranha infested waters?**

I'd do it for free

☑ **HYP**

☐ 0.0%

$50

☐ 1.5%

$1000

☐ 3.0%

$50,000

☐ 1.5%

$1,000,000

▭ 24.1%

I would never do it

▭ 69.9%

Responses: 133

☒ **Generally, what is an appropriate amount to tip a waiter/waitress?**

5%

☐ 5.3%

10%

▭ 15.9%

15%

▭ 62.3%

20%

▭ 14.6%

None of the above

☐ 2.0%

Responses: 151

☒ **How do you think you compare (or will compare) to your parents in terms of financial success?**

More successful

▭ 44.2%

About the same

▭ 39.2%

Not as successful

☐ 16.7%

Responses: 120

☒What is the least amount of money you would stop to pick up if you saw it on the sidewalk?

One penny

☐ 40.6%   ☑HYP

Five cents

☐ 18.1%

A dime

☐ 8.7%

A quarter

☐ 21.7%

A dollar

☐ 6.5%

None of the above

☐ 4.3%

Responses: 138

☒What do you normally use to pay for your purchases?

Debit card

☐ 39.4%

Cash

☐ 29.1%

Credit card

☐ 18.9%

Check

☐ 12.6%

Responses: 127

☒If you were offered $50 to attend a two hour time-share presentation, would you do it?

Yes

☐ 35.1%   ☑HYP

No

[====================] 56.0%

I'm not sure

[□] 9.0%

Responses: 134

☒ Have you refinanced your home recently?

-Poll Date: 20-Jun-2003

Yes

[=========] 29.1%

No, but I'm planning on it

[□] 11.8%

No

[=========] 29.1%

I don't have a house

[=========] 30.0%

Responses: 110

☒ What is the least amount of money you would sell one of your kidneys for?

$1000

[□] 3.1%   ☑ HYP

$10,000

[□] 1.5%

$100,000

[□] 9.2%

$1,000,000

[=====] 16.9%

More than a million

[=====] 15.4%

I would never sell one of my kidneys

[==================] 53.8%

Responses: 65

☒If you won the lottery jackpot, would you take the smaller lump-sum or receive installments for the full amount over the next 30 years?

Lump-sum

☑HYP

66.7%

Installments

33.3%

Responses: 69

☒What is the least amount of money you would sell your right arm for?

1 million dollars

☑HYP

☐   0.0%

5 million dollars

☐   1.5%

10 million dollars

☐   4.4%

50 million dollars

☐   2.9%

100 million dollars

13.2%

I would never sell my right arm

77.9%

Responses: 68

☒Do you have a personal acquaintance who is a millionaire?

Yes

35.5%

No

53.9%

I'm not sure

10.5%

Responses: 76

☒ What amount would you consider "making good money" to be?
-Poll Date: 12-Sep-2003

$50,000/year
☐ 13.0%

$75,000/year
☐ 18.0%

$100,000/year
☐ 36.0%

$125,000/year
☐ 8.0%

$150,000/year
☐ 21.0%

None of the above
☐ 4.0%

Responses: 100

☒ How much credit card debt do you have?

None
☐ 36.9%

Less than $1000
☐ 21.5%

$1000–$2000
☐ 7.7%

$2000–$3000
☐ 3.1%

$3000–$4000
☐ 3.1%

$4000–$5000
☐ 4.6%

More than $5000
☐ 23.1%

Responses: 65

☒ Do you like to get a sales receipt for small purchases?

No, I don't need the receipt
☐ 43.9%

Yes, I like to have the receipt even for small purchases

| | 51.0%

I'm not sure

▢ 5.1%

Responses: 98

☒ How do you feel about your wages?

-Poll Date: 15-Nov-2003

Fairly compensated

| | 28.1%

Underpaid

| | 29.7%

Overpaid

▢ 0.0%

I'm self employed

▢ 7.8%

I don't have a job

| | 34.4%

Responses: 64

☒ What is the most you would pay for a pair of jeans?

Less than $20

| | 25.2%

$40

| | 50.5%

$60

| | 18.4%

More than $60

▢ 5.8%

Responses: 103

☒ Would you rather volunteer time or give money?

Time

| | 45.1%

Money

| | 43.1%

Neither

11.8%

Responses: 102

☒ How good is your credit?

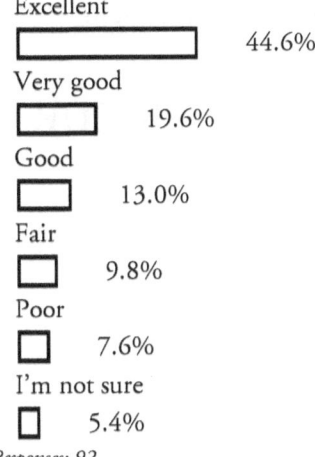

Excellent

44.6%

Very good

19.6%

Good

13.0%

Fair

9.8%

Poor

7.6%

I'm not sure

5.4%

Responses: 92

☒ How good are you at budgeting your money?

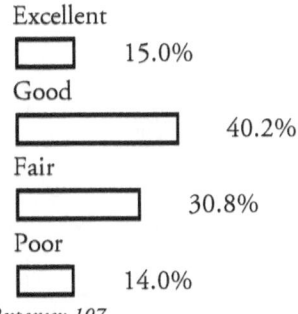

Excellent

15.0%

Good

40.2%

Fair

30.8%

Poor

14.0%

Responses: 107

News Stories

☒ **What should they do with the D.C. Sniper once he is caught?**
-Poll Date: 22-Oct-2002

Death by firing squad
☐ 76.7%   ☑**CUR**

Give him life in prison
☐ 17.5%

Submit him to a mental institution
☐ 5.8%

Responses: 120

☒ **Do you feel threatened by the new sickness called SARS?**
-Poll Date: 10-Apr-2003

Yes
☐ 16.1%   ☑**CUR**

No
☐ 70.1%

I'm not sure
☐ 13.9%

Responses: 137

☒ **Is Martha Stewart getting what she deserves?**
-Poll Date: 07-Jun-2003

Yes
☐ 45.8%   ☑**CUR**

No
☐ 23.6%

I'm not sure
☐ 30.6%

Responses: 72

☒ Should the U.S. send troops to Liberia?

-Poll Date: 17-Jul-2003

Yes

☑ **CUR**

18.2%

No

51.1%

I'm not sure

30.7%

Responses: 88

☒ How big of factor do you think race will be in the Kobe Bryant case?

-Poll Date: 10-Aug-2003

Very big

☑ **CUR**

13.1%

Moderately big

13.1%

Somewhat big

9.8%

Not very big

57.4%

I'm not sure

6.6%

Responses: 61

Personal

☒ **Do you believe in the existence of extraterrestrial beings?**

Most definitely
59.4%

I'm not really sure
18.9%

Absolutely not
21.7%

Responses: 106

☒ **How would you rate your own looks compared to your peers?**

Greatly above average
3.9%

Moderately above average
19.4%

A little above average
22.6%

Average
31.0%

A little below average
12.9%

Moderately below average
6.1%

Greatly below average
4.2%

Responses: 310

☒ **Which of these would be the best accolade to receive?**

Best personality
46.6%

Most talented

24.1%

Most likely to succeed

22.4%

Most attractive

4.3%

Most athletic

2.6%

Responses: 116

☒What type of weather do you like best?

Clear

49.5%   ☑**FAV**

Thunder and lightning

15.0%

Snowy

13.1%

Partly cloudy

11.2%

Rainy

10.3%

Windy

0.9%

Responses: 107

☒If you could choose your path to fame, what would you be?

Renown expert on a certain field of study   ☑**HYP**

26.7%

Lead singer for a famous band

25.2%

Movie star

23.7%

CEO of a fortune 500 company

13.7%

Star athlete for a professional team

10.7%

Responses: 131

☒What would be the worst way to die?

Burning

| | 69.3%

Sickness

| | 12.5%

Drowning

| | 12.5%

Hanging

□ 4.5%

Being shot

□ 1.1%

Responses: 88

☒How would your rate your penmanship?

Excellent

□ 8.0%

Good

| | 36.2%

Ok

| | 28.3%

Not so good

| | 15.9%

Really bad

| | 11.6%

Responses: 138

☒What is the most powerful motivational force?

Love

| | 50.6%

Money

| | 28.7%

Praise

□ 6.9%

Peer pressure

□ 6.9%

Criticism

☐   2.3%

Other

☐   4.6%

Responses: 87

☒Are you a morning person?

Yes

[   ]   27.0%

Somewhat

[   ]   31.8%

No

[   ]   41.2%

Responses: 148

☒Which one of these traits best describes you?

Easy going

[   ]   37.0%

Analytical

[   ]   25.3%

Compassionate

[   ]   14.4%

Organized

☐   9.6%

Outgoing

☐   9.6%

Confident

☐   4.1%

Responses: 146

☒What do you read the most?

Online content

[   ]   32.9%

Books

[   ]   28.1%

Newspapers

☐ 21.2%

Magazines

☐ 17.8%

Responses: 146

☒What side of your brain is dominate?

Left (Logical)

☐ 55.2%

Right (Creative)

☐ 15.6%

They're both about even

☐ 29.2%

Responses: 96

☒Are you a cat person or a dog person?

Cat

☐ 20.7%

Dog

☐ 43.3%

Neither

☐ 7.3%

I like both about the same

☐ 28.7%

Responses: 150

☒Are you an organ donor?

Yes

☐ 51.8%

No

☐ 48.2%

Responses: 137

☒How often to you wear perfume/cologne?

Every day

☐ 21.3%

Several times a week

26.3%

Several times a month

1.3%

Only on special occasions

27.5%

Never

23.8%

Responses: 80

☒ How patriotic are you?

Very

55.9%

Somewhat

29.0%

A little

13.1%

Not at all

2.1%

Responses: 145

☒ Would you ever go bungee jumping off a tall bridge?

You Bet!

19.1%

☑ HYP

No Way!

62.9%

I'm not sure

18.0%

Responses: 89

☒ Which one of these personality types do you consider yourself to be?

Introverted

26.2%

Extroverted

☐ 20.6%

In between the two

☐ 53.2%

Responses: 126

☒ How often do you shampoo your hair?

Every day

☐ 52.1%

Several times a week

☐ 37.5%

Once a week

☐ 7.3%

Less than once a week

☐ 3.1%

Responses: 96

☒ What do you consider your intelligence to be?

Greatly above average

☐ 15.1%

Moderately above average

☐ 56.8%

Average

☐ 26.0%

Moderately below average

☐ 2.1%

Greatly below average

☐ 0.0%

Responses: 146

☒ How often do you experience insomnia?

Frequently

☐ 20.8%

Every once in a while

☐ 40.8%

Almost never

33.6%

Never

4.8%

Responses: 125

☒ How do you feel about winning and losing?

I like winning more than I dislike losing

44.5%

I like to win about as much as I dislike losing

21.1%

I'm indifferent

18.0%

I hate losing more than I like winning

16.4%

Responses: 128

☒ What creature scares you the most?

Snake

33.8%

Rat

24.3%

Spider

19.1%

Bee

5.1%

Bat

3.7%

None of the above

14.0%

Responses: 136

☒ What position do you normally sleep in?

Side

67.2%

Stomach

☐ 18.2%

Back

☐ 14.6%

Responses: 137

☒Are you afraid of flying?

Yes

☐ 19.3%

No

☐ 80.7%

Responses: 88

☒Do you have your own web site?

Yes

☐ 13.0%

No

☐ 71.5%

No, but I would like to have one

☐ 15.4%

Responses: 123

☒Would you rather be a super athlete or a super model?

Super athlete

☐ 65.7%   ☑HYP

Super model

☐ 34.3%

Responses: 108

☒Would you take a flight to outer space if you could afford it?

Yes

☐ 37.0%   ☑HYP

No, I wouldn't waste my money on it

☐ 32.8%

No, I would be afraid to

☐☐☐☐☐ 25.2%

I'm not sure

☐ 5.0%

Responses: 119

☒What kind of watch do you prefer?

Analog

☐☐☐☐☐☐☐ 66.1%

Digital

☐☐☐ 19.4%

I don't like to wear a watch

☐☐ 14.5%

Responses: 124

☒Are you more of a leader, a follower, or are you more independent?

Independent

☐☐☐☐☐☐☐☐ 73.3%

Leader

☐☐ 16.2%

Follower

☐ 10.5%

Responses: 105

☒How much do you care about what others think of you?

Greatly

☐ 9.5%

Quite a bit

☐☐☐ 24.3%

Somewhat

☐☐☐☐ 36.5%

A little

☐☐☐ 20.3%

Not at all

☐ 9.5%

Responses: 74

☒ **How would you rate your self esteem?**

5-Very High
☐ 8.3%

4
▭ 37.0%

3
▭ 37.0%

2
▭ 13.0%

1-Very Low
☐ 4.6%

Responses: 108

☒ **How do you normally respond when someone does something to irritate you?**

With direct and frank communication
▭ 24.8%

With complaints about them to others
▭ 19.8%

With patience and tolerance
▭ 19.8%

With tactful and polite communication
▭ 15.8%

With an angry confrontation
☐ 8.9%

Other
☐ 10.9%

Responses: 101

☒ **How often do you use deodorant?**

Every day
▭ 84.3%

About every other day
☐ 6.1%

Once a week

☐ 0.9%

Less than once a week

☐ 4.3%

Responses: 115

☒ Do you wear glasses?

Yes

[▭] 45.5%

No, I wear contacts

[▭] 22.3%

No, but I should

[▭] 11.6%

No, I don't need glasses

[▭] 20.5%

Responses: 112

☒ Have you ever had your identity stolen?

Yes

☐ 4.3%

No

[▭] 90.2%

Possibly, I'm not sure

☐ 5.4%

Responses: 92

☒ Have you ever skipped to the last page of a novel to find out how it ends?

Yes

[▭] 43.7%

No

[▭] 56.3%

Responses: 71

☒What is the most repulsive pet?

Rat

30.0%

Tarantula

20.0%

Snake

20.0%

Skunk

11.8%

Piranha

5.5%

Alligator

4.5%

Lizard

2.7%

Other

5.5%

Responses: 110

☒Would you like to know what others truly think about you?

Yes

41.2%

No

36.8%

I'm not sure

22.1%

Responses: 68

☒Do you brown nose?

Yes

7.5%

A little, I suppose

47.5%

No

45.0%

Responses: 80

☒ What color of hair do you like most?

I'm indifferent

☐ 29.6%

Brown

☐ 20.4%

Blond

☐ 19.4%

Red

☐ 19.4%

Black

☐ 11.1%

Responses: 108

☒ How often do you look at yourself in the mirror?

1–5 times a day

☐ 70.3%

6–10 times a day

☐ 12.2%

11–15 times a day

☐ 12.2%

16–20 times a day

☐ 2.7%

More than 20 times a day

☐ 2.7%

Responses: 74

☒ How would you rate your responsibility?

1-Very responsible

☐ 38.0%

2

☐ 42.3%

3

☐ 15.5%

4

☐ 4.2%

5-Very irresponsible

☐ 0.0%

Responses: 71

☒ How well do you sing?

Very good

☐ 7.5%

Good

☐ 15.1%

Fair

☐ 21.7%

Not very good

☐ 30.2%

Pretty bad

☐ 25.5%

Responses: 106

☒ How are you doing today?

Great

☐ 19.6%

Good

☐ 32.4%

Ok

☐ 35.3%

Not so good

☐ 9.8%

Terrible

☐ 2.9%

Responses: 102

☒ What kind of foot wear do you prefer wearing?

Athletic Shoes

☐ 41.0%

Sandals

☐ 30.0%

Casual Shoes

☐ 19.0%

Boots

☐ 6.0%

Dress Shoes

☐ 3.0%

Other

☐ 1.0%

Responses: 100

☒What is your favorite season?

Fall

☐ 30.9%

Winter

☐ 5.9%

Spring

☐ 30.9%

Summer

☐ 32.4%

Responses: 68

☒Do you have unused exercise equipment at your house?

Yes

☐ 48.2%

No, I don't have exercise equipment

☐ 43.4%

No, I use my exercise equipment

☐ 8.4%

Responses: 83

☒If you could choose your eye color, what would it be?

Blue

☐ 42.1%

Green

☐ 29.0%

Brown

☐　　16.8%

Hazel

☐　　12.1%

Responses: 107

☒What do you do most during your free time?

Watch T.V.

☐　　37.5%

Hobbies

☐　　16.7%

Read

☐　　11.5%

Chores

☐　　9.4%

Athletics

☐　　6.3%

Sleep

☐　　4.2%

Other

☐　　14.6%

Responses: 96

☒If you were in a rock band, what part would you want to play?

Lead singer

☐　　29.6%　　　　　　　　　　☑HYP

Drummer

☐　　21.7%

Keyboard player

☐　　19.1%

Guitarist

☐　　19.1%

Bass guitarist

☐　　10.4%

Responses: 115

☒How often do you exercise?

Every day
☐   7.4%

A few times a week
▭ 26.5%

Once in a while
▭ 26.5%

Almost never
▭ 26.5%

Never
☐ 13.2%

Responses: 68

☒If you could improve yourself in some way, which would it be?

I would have more money
▭ 28.3%

I would be more attractive
▭ 18.9%

I would be more intelligent
▭ 17.0%

I would be more spiritual
▭ 16.0%

I would be more talented
▭ 11.3%

I would be more popular
☐ 1.9%

Other
☐ 6.6%

Responses: 106

☒What is your stance on abortion?

Pro-choice
▭ 42.9%

☑CON

Pro-life
▭ 40.2%

Neither/Undecided

[   ]   17.0%

Responses: 112

☒Are you more of a fix-it-yourself person or would you rather have someone else do it?

Fix-it-yourself

[   ]   31.9%

Have someone else do it

[   ]   36.1%

A little of both

[   ]   31.9%

Responses: 72

☒Which of these pets would you most like to have?

Dog

[   ]   61.1%

Cat

[   ]   33.7%

Bird

[ ]   3.2%

Rabbit

[ ]   2.1%

Responses: 95

☒Which do you believe in: evolution or creationism?

Evolution

[   ]   34.7%

☑CON

Creationism

[   ]   29.3%

Both

[   ]   36.0%

Neither

[ ]   0.0%

Responses: 75

☒ How long does it take you to get ready in the morning?

Less than 15 minutes
☐   10.8%

15 to 30 minutes
☐   40.2%

30 minutes to 1 hour
☐   40.2%

1 to 2 hours
☐   8.8%

More than 2 hours
☐   0.0%

Responses: 102

☒ Are you superstitious?

Yes
☐   34.4%

No
☐   65.6%

Responses: 61

☒ Have you ever seen the future in a dream?

Yes
☐   47.7%   ☑ **FUT**

No
☐   52.3%

Responses: 65

☒ How often do you use the internet?

Less than 1 hour a week
☐   0.0%

1 to 5 hours a week
☐   10.7%

5 to 10 hours a week
☐   28.6%

More than 10 hours

▭ 60.7%

Responses: 56

☒How would you rate your manners compared to those of your peers?

Greatly above average

▭ 20.8%

Moderately above average

▭ 47.2%

Average

▭ 30.6%

Moderately below average

☐ 1.4%

Greatly below average

☐ 0.0%

Responses: 72

☒Rate how important it is for you to be well dressed.

5-Very important

▭ 11.6%

4

▭ 27.4%

3-Somewhat important

▭ 46.3%

2

☐ 9.5%

1-Not at all important

☐ 5.3%

Responses: 95

☒Is anger a voluntary or an involuntary reaction?

Voluntary

▭ 23.2%

Involuntary

▭ 21.2%

Could be either

| | 55.6%

Responses: 99

☒Are people really as tall as they say they are?

Yes, most of the time

| | 36.2%

No, they're usually about an inch shorter

| | 55.3%

No, they're usually about two inches shorter

☐ 3.2%

No, they're usually taller

☐ 0.0%

I'm not sure

☐ 5.3%

Responses: 94

☒If NASA offered you a free tourist trip to space, would you take it?

Yes

| | 48.0%   ☑HYP

No

| | 52.0%

Responses: 75

☒How much do you like little kids?

Very much

| | 26.3%

Quite a bit

| | 30.3%

Somewhat

| | 22.4%

A little

| | 15.8%

Not at all

☐ 5.3%

Responses: 76

☒ How well do you take criticism?

Much better than most people

☐ 6.9%

A little better than most people

▭ 23.8%

About the same as everyone else

▭ 52.5%

Not quite as well as most people

▭ 15.8%

Much worse than most people

☐ 1.0%

Responses: 101

☒ How many people do you think hide a dark secret?

Everyone

▭ 15.2%

Almost everyone

▭ 54.3%

Some

▭ 27.6%

Few

☐ 1.9%

Hardly anyone

☐ 1.0%

Responses: 105

☒ How would you rate your athleticism compared to your peers?

Greatly above average

☐ 3.1%

Moderately above average

▭ 21.5%

Average

▭ 29.2%

Moderately below average

▭ 23.1%

Greatly below average

[bar] 23.1%

Responses: 65

☒Are you a control freak?

Yes

[bar] 17.8%

No

[bar] 34.2%

Maybe a little

[bar] 47.9%

Responses: 73

☒Would it be worse to be obese or stupid?

Stupid

[bar] 68.5%

Obese

[bar] 31.5%

Responses: 111

☒Would you go to a nude beach?

I'm male—I would go

[bar] 41.7%

I'm male—I would not go

[bar] 58.3%

Male Responses: 48

I'm female—I would go

[bar] 23.4%

I'm female—I would not go

[bar] 76.6%

Female Responses: 47

☒How often do you make your bed?

Everyday

[bar] 34.8%

Almost everyday
13.0%

Every now and then
18.8%

Seldom
17.4%

Never
15.9%

Responses: 69

☒ How do you come up with a password?

With a mixture of familiar numbers and letters
26.1%

With a random word
14.8%

With a pet's name
10.2%

With a person's name
6.8%

With a familiar number
5.7%

With a personal event
4.5%

With a random number
2.3%

Other
29.5%

Responses: 88

☒ What do you like more: sleeping or eating?

Sleeping
38.4%

Eating
32.1%

They're too close to choose

☐ 29.5%

Responses: 112

☒ **What is the most distant relationship you could have with someone in order to give them one of your kidneys to save their life?**

Immediate family

☐ 22.4%   ☑ **HYP**

Extended family

☐ 8.2%

Close friend

☐ 40.8%

Acquaintance

☐ 4.1%

Stranger

☐ 19.4%

I wouldn't give one of my kidneys

☐ 5.1%

Responses: 98

☒ **How do you feel about where you are in life?**

The best years are behind me

☐ 18.8%

I'm in the best years

☐ 35.6%

The best years are still ahead of me

☐ 45.5%

Responses: 101

☒ **Rate how good of a speller you are.**

1-Excellent

☐ 35.7%

2

☐ 35.7%

3-Fair

☐ 18.6%

4

□ 7.1%

5-Very poor

□ 2.9%

Responses: 70

☒How much do you worry?

1-Worry wart

[▭] 17.6%

2

[▭] 12.2%

3-Average

[▭] 35.1%

4

[▭] 29.7%

5-Carefree

□ 5.4%

Responses: 74

☒How strong is your work ethic?

1-Very strong

[▭] 36.5%

2

[▭] 33.3%

3-Fairly strong

[▭] 14.6%

4

□ 7.3%

5-Not very strong at all

□ 8.3%

Responses: 96

☒Who or what has the greatest influence on a person's behavior?

Parents

[▭] 42.4%

One's self

34.3%

Peers

17.2%

Religion

4.0%

Media

2.0%

Responses: 99

☒What is the greatest amount of physical pain you have experienced?

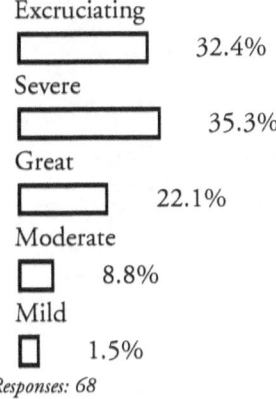

Excruciating

32.4%

Severe

35.3%

Great

22.1%

Moderate

8.8%

Mild

1.5%

Responses: 68

☒How many times have you cried in the past month?

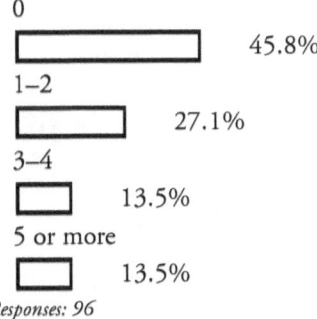

0

45.8%

1–2

27.1%

3–4

13.5%

5 or more

13.5%

Responses: 96

☒ Do you have any regrets?

Yes, major regrets

☐ 40.0%

Yes, minor regrets

☐ 50.0%

No

☐ 10.0%

Responses: 100

Race

☒ How do blacks compare to other races athletically?

More athletic

[bar] 62.9%

About the same as other races

[bar] 31.8%

Less athletic

[ ] 2.6%

I'm not sure

[ ] 2.6%

Responses: 151

☒ Has Affirmative Action unintentionally resulted in reverse discrimination?

-Poll Date: 04-Dec-2002

Often times, yes

[bar] 44.3% ☑ CON

Sometimes, yes

[bar] 39.7% ☑ CUR

Very rarely

[ ] 4.6%

No

[ ] 3.8%

I'm not sure

[ ] 7.6%

Responses: 131

☒ Should blacks receive reparations for civil rights crimes against their ancestors?

-Poll Date: 17-Jan-2003

Yes

[ ] 4.5% ☑ CON

No

88.3%   ☑CUR

I'm not sure

☐ 7.1%

Responses: 154

☒What do you think about college admission policies that give extra points to minorities?

-Poll Date: 20-Jan-2003

They are well intentioned, but have flaws

43.0%   ☑CON

They are a very bad idea

38.8%   ☑CUR

They could probably use some adjustments

☐ 12.4%

I'm indifferent

☐ 4.1%

They are a very good idea

☐ 1.7%

Responses: 121

☒What racial group is most discriminated against?

Blacks

31.2%

Whites

27.2%

Arabs

25.6%

Hispanics

☐ 4.0%

Asians

☐ 2.4%

Other

☐ 9.6%

Responses: 125

☒Should minorities receive extra points for admission into college?

Yes
☐ 7.1%

No
▭ 85.8%

I'm not sure
☐ 7.1%

Responses: 141

☒Why are there so few black coaches in college and professional football?

Lack of qualified candidates
▭ 50.9%

Racism
▭ 19.3%

I'm not sure
▭ 29.8%

Responses: 114

☒What factor do you think is most common in discriminatory hiring practices?

Physical appearance
▭ 45.4%

Age
▭ 19.9%

Race
▭ 13.5%

Sex
☐ 12.1%

Disability
☐ 8.5%

Other
☐ 0.7%

Responses: 141

☒ Do you approve of interracial marriages?

Yes

61.8%

No

28.2%

I'm not sure

9.9%

Responses: 131

☒ Has America become hypersensitive to race?

Yes

77.8%

No

6.7%

I'm not sure

15.6%

Responses: 90

☒ How do you feel about the use of "hyphenated Americans" (e.g. "African-American" or "European-American")?

Political correctness gone too far

34.9%

Promotes unhealthy division of Americans

27.0%

I'm indifferent

25.4%

It's appropriate and respectful

12.7%

Responses: 63

☒ If you could trade places with someone from a different race for a day, would you do it?

Yes

45.5%

☑ HYP

No

42.7%

I'm not sure

11.8%

Responses: 110

☒Will racial problems increase or decrease in the future?

Increase

27.7%

Decrease

40.6%

Neither, they will stay the same

26.7%

I'm not sure

5.0%

Responses: 101

☑**FUT**

Relationships and Dating

☒**Should gay people be allowed to marry?**
-Poll Date: 12-Dec-2002

Yes
| | 44.5%

No
| | 46.6%

I'm not sure
☐ 8.9%

Responses: 146

☑CUR

☑CON

☒**What do you notice first when you meet someone?**

Eyes
| | 41.7%

Physique
| | 34.8%

Hair
☐ 6.1%

Mouth
☐ 6.1%

Voice
☐ 2.3%

Other
☐ 9.1%

Responses: 132

☒**Is it okay for the woman to propose?**

Yes
| | 69.1%

No
| | 22.8%

I'm not sure

☐   8.1%

Responses: 136

☒What is the best age to get married?

-Poll Date: 18-Mar-2003

18–20

☐   0.0%

21–23

☐   10.1%

24–26

55.1%

27–29

18.8%

30+

15.9%

Responses: 138

☒Is it okay to kiss on the first date?

Yes, always

☐   10.5%

Yes, usually

☐   12.6%

It depends on how the date went

64.3%

Not usually

☐   8.4%

No, it's never okay

☐   4.2%

Responses: 143

☒What part of the face is most important in measuring attractiveness?

Eyes

50.0%

Smile

36.0%

Nose

6.0%

Cheeks

2.7%

Lips

2.7%

Other

2.7%

Responses: 150

☒ Do you believe there is a soul mate for everyone?

Yes

51.2%

No

37.8%

I'm not sure

11.0%

Responses: 82

☒ If your spouse was a movie star, would it bother you if he/she kissed someone else in a movie?

Yes, greatly

20.0%

☑ HYP

I would be somewhat bothered

22.9%

Maybe just a little

33.3%

No, I wouldn't be bothered at all

23.8%

Responses: 105

☒ **Rate how important you think physical attraction is in choosing a partner?**

7-Very important
☐   11.2%

6
☐   20.4%

5
☐   33.7%

4-Somewhat important
☐   29.6%

3
☐ 3.1%

2
☐ 1.0%

1-Not at all important
☐ 1.0%

Responses: 98

☒ **What percentage of married couples do you think remain faithful to each other throughout their marriages?**

0 to 20%
☐   12.9%

20 to 40%
☐   24.1%

40 to 60%
☐   31.9%

60 to 80%
☐   29.3%

80 to 100%
☐ 1.7%

Responses: 116

☒ **Where is the best place to find a significant other?**

Church
☐   30.7%

School

17.8%

Work

16.8%

Bar

2.0%

Elsewhere

32.7%

Responses: 101

☒When a woman dates a younger man, when does the age difference make the relationship inappropriate?

Never

46.6%

When she is 1 to 3 years older than him

0.0%

When she is 4 to 6 years older than him

9.6%

When she is 7 to 9 years older than him

9.6%

When she is 10 or more years older than him

34.2%

Responses: 73

☒When a man dates a younger woman, when does the age difference make the relationship inappropriate?

Never

47.9%

When he is 1 to 3 years older than her

0.0%

When he is 4 to 6 years older than her

4.2%

When he is 7 to 9 years older than her

5.6%

When he is 10 or more years older than her

| | 42.3%
Responses: 71

☒Can you tell how attractive someone is just by listening to their voice?

Yes

| | 16.5%

No

| | 77.1%

I'm not sure

☐ 6.4%
Responses: 109

☒Does smoking make a difference in how attractive someone is?

No, it doesn't make a difference

| | 12.7%

Yes, they become less attractive

| | 87.3%

Yes, they become more attractive

☐ 0.0%
Responses: 71

☒What do you do if you are meeting someone for the first time and you notice that they have a piece of food stuck in their teeth?

Try to ignore it

| | 59.0%   ☑HYP

Tell them they have something in their teeth

| | 39.0%

Bolt

☐ 1.9%
Responses: 105

☒Are you more likely to break hearts or be heart broken?

Be heart broken

| | 74.8%

Break hearts

[_____]   25.2%

Responses: 103

☒ Would you rather be married or single?

Married

[_____]   66.1%

Single

[_____]   14.8%

I'm not sure

[_____]   19.1%

Responses: 115

☒ Is it okay to flirt if you are married?

Yes, there's no harm in it

[_____]   14.4%

Maybe just a little

[_____]   40.7%

No, it could lead to something more serious

[_____]   8.5%

No, it's disloyal to your spouse

[_____]   32.2%

I'm not sure

[___]   4.2%

Responses: 118

☒ Is it appropriate for a woman to keep her maiden name after marriage?

Yes

[_____]   41.6%

Maybe under special circumstances

[_____]   35.6%

No

[_____]   22.8%

Responses: 101

☒Do nice guys really finish last?

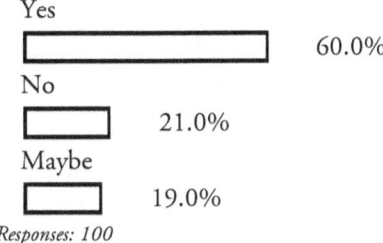

Yes, it's true
43.6%

No way
56.4%

Responses: 110

☒Can teenagers experience true love?

Yes
60.0%

No
21.0%

Maybe
19.0%

Responses: 100

☒Should a pill similar to Viagra be made for women?
-Poll Date: 19-Jan-2004

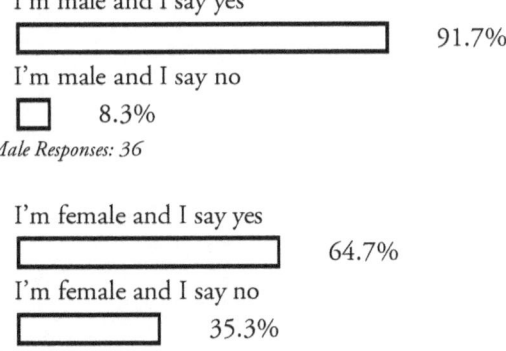

I'm male and I say yes
91.7%

I'm male and I say no
8.3%

Male Responses: 36

I'm female and I say yes
64.7%

I'm female and I say no
35.3%

Female Responses: 51

Religion and Spirituality

☒ How do you feel about celebrating religious holidays (like Christmas) in schools?

In favor

66.1%

Opposed

17.7%

I'm indifferent

16.1%

Responses: 62

☒ How do you feel about removing "Christ" from "Christmas" for political correctness?

It's a very bad idea

78.3%   ☑CON

Why change, its not hurting anyone

14.1%

I'm indifferent

3.3%

It's a very good idea

3.3%

It should probably be changed

1.1%

Responses: 92

☒ Is there only one true religion?

Yes

34.0%   ☑CON

No

59.8%

I'm not sure

☐ 6.2%

Responses: 97

☒What is your view of the Muslim scripture, the Quran?

It contains good teachings, but they are interpreted incorrectly

☐ 34.4%

It is a true book with righteous teachings

☐ 11.5%

It is an evil book

☐ 6.1%

It has no great significance

☐ 4.6%

It promotes terrorism

☐ 3.8%

I'm not sure

☐ 39.7%

Responses: 131

☒Do you believe in divine intervention?

Yes

☐ 73.3%

No

☐ 14.4%

I'm not sure

☐ 12.2%

Responses: 90

☒Are good works required for salvation?

Yes

☐ 37.6%

No

☐ 34.4%

I'm not sure

☐ 12.9%

☑CON

I wouldn't know, I'm not religious

☐   15.1%

Responses: 93

☒Should the phrase "under God" be removed from the Pledge of Allegiance?

-Poll Date: 08-Mar-2003

Yes

☐   17.0%   ☑**CUR**

No

☐   79.8%   ☑**CON**

I'm not sure

☐   3.2%

Responses: 94

☒How important is religion to you?

Very important

☐   35.5%

Somewhat important

☐   29.0%

Not very important

☐   15.1%

Not at all important

☐   20.4%

Responses: 93

☒Do you believe in guardian angels?

Yes

☐   58.3%

No

☐   27.2%

I'm not sure

☐   14.6%

Responses: 103

☒Should the Ten Commandments be removed from public buildings?

-Poll Date: 20-Aug-2003

Yes

☐ 14.3%

No

76.5%

I'm not sure

☐ 9.2%

Responses: 98

☑CUR

☑CON

☒Are prayers really answered?

Yes

63.6%

No

23.4%

I'm not sure

☐ 13.0%

Responses: 77

☒Do you believe that each person has an aura?

Yes

53.7%

No

23.9%

I'm not sure

22.4%

Responses: 67

☒What percentage of your income do you spend on charity?

Less than 1%

51.5%

1–3%

26.7%

4–6%

☐   6.9%

7–9%

☐   7.9%

10% or more

☐   6.9%

Responses: 101

☒Is there life after death?

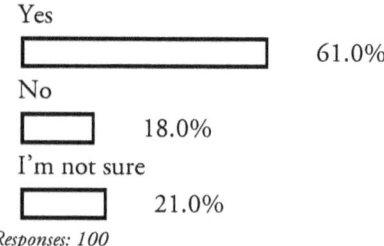

Yes

61.0%

No

18.0%

I'm not sure

21.0%

Responses: 100

☒Is it possible to communicate with spirits?

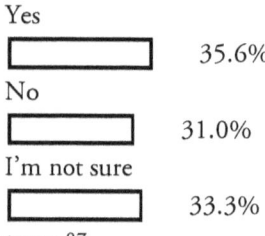

Yes

35.6%

No

31.0%

I'm not sure

33.3%

Responses: 87

School

☒ **What kind of grades did you/do you get in high school?**

Straight As
☐ 6.0%

As and Bs
[▮] 49.3%

Bs and Cs
[▮] 35.8%

Cs and Ds
☐ 9.0%

Responses: 67

☒ **Should schools install video cameras in classrooms?**

Yes
[▮] 51.5%   ☑ CON

No
[▮] 40.4%

I'm not sure
☐ 8.1%

Responses: 99

☒ **What is the minimum level of education needed in order to be successful?**

High school diploma
[▮] 27.1%

Associate Degree
☐ 3.7%

Bachelor's Degree
[▮] 25.2%

Master's Degree
☐ 7.5%

Doctorate

☐   0.0%

There is no minimum

[▭]   36.4%

Responses: 107

☒What is the most boring subject?

English

[▭]   45.5%   ☑**COM**

Math

[▭]   36.4%

History

[▭]   11.7%

Science

☐   6.5%

Responses: 77

☒How do you prefer to learn something new?

By having someone else teach me

☐   10.8%

By figuring it out myself

[▭]   14.9%

A mixture of both

[▭]   74.3%

Responses: 74

☒Should sex education courses emphasize contraception or abstinence?

Contraception

☐   9.9%   ☑**CON**

Abstinence

[▭]   28.7%

Both

[▭]   61.4%

Responses: 101

Society and Culture

☒**What is the most courteous region in the U.S.?**

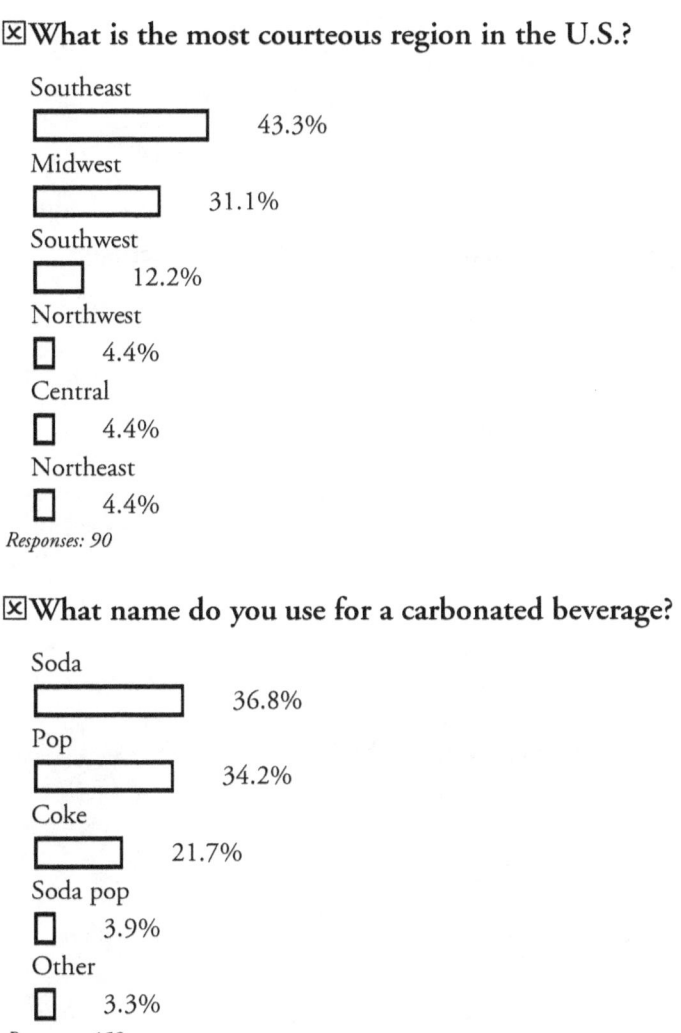

Southeast

43.3%

Midwest

31.1%

Southwest

12.2%

Northwest

4.4%

Central

4.4%

Northeast

4.4%

Responses: 90

☒**What name do you use for a carbonated beverage?**

Soda

36.8%

Pop

34.2%

Coke

21.7%

Soda pop

3.9%

Other

3.3%

Responses: 152

☒**What do you think about smoking in public areas?**

It's inconsiderate

☑**COM**

[bar] 39.6%

It doesn't bother me

[bar] 26.4%

It's very rude

[bar] 20.8%

There is no problem with it

[bar] 13.2%

Responses: 144

☒**What comes to your mind when you think of British accents?**

Proper

[bar] 35.0%

Endearing

[bar] 18.7%

Snooty

[bar] 17.9%

I wish I had one

[bar] 16.3%

Annoying

[bar] 12.2%

Responses: 123

☒**If you could speak another language, which would it be?**

Spanish

[bar] 50.0%

French

[bar] 21.3%

German

[bar] 11.3%

Japanese

[bar] 6.3%

Russian

[bar] 3.8%

Arabic

☐ 1.3%

Hebrew

☐ 1.3%

Other

☐ 5.0%

Responses: 80

Sports

☒**How do you feel about the end of the college football season?**
-Poll Date: 05-Jan-2003

It was time for it to end
☐ 30.8%
I'm glad it's over
☐ 14.3%
I wish it could have gone on longer
☐ 9.9%
What college football season?
☐ 45.1%

Responses: 91

☑**CUR**

☒**What did you like best about the Super Bowl?**
-Poll Date: 27-Jan-2003

The commercials
☐ 31.1%
The game
☐ 25.0%
The friends
☐ 4.7%
The food
☐ 3.4%
I didn't watch the Super Bowl
☐ 35.8%

Responses: 148

☑**CUR**

☒**Who should finance professional sports stadiums: team owners or tax payers?**

The team owners
☐ 53.6%

Both, the owner paying the majority

| 37.6%

Both, the tax payers paying the majority

□ 4.8%

The tax payers

□ 4.0%

Responses: 125

⊠Do you consider cheerleading to be a sport?

Yes

| 32.5%

No

| 64.9%

I'm not sure

□ 2.6%

Responses: 77

☑**CON**

⊠Should girls be allowed to play football?

Yes

| 68.4%

No

| 29.8%

I'm not sure

□ 1.8%

Responses: 114

☑**CON**

⊠What sport is the most physically demanding?

Football

| 21.8%

Soccer

| 21.8%

Water Polo

| 20.8%

Wrestling

| 11.9%

Running
☐ 10.9%
Basketball
☐ 8.9%
Other
☐ 4.0%
Responses: 101

☒Do you plan on watching the women's soccer world cup?
-Poll Date: 22-Sep-2003

No, I'm not interested in watching soccer
☐ 69.8%   ☑CUR
No, I'm not interested in watching women's sports
☐ 9.4%
Yes, I like to watch all soccer matches
☐ 5.2%
Yes, only because its the world championship
☐ 4.2%
Yes, only if my team advances to the final
☐ 3.1%
I'm not sure
☐ 8.3%
Responses: 96

☒Are you a hunter?

Yes
☐ 17.1%
No
☐ 82.9%
Responses: 111

☒How do you feel about the Yankees?

Love 'em!
☐ 14.4%
Hate 'em!
☐ 27.0%

I'm indifferent

58.6%

Responses: 111

☒ **Which of these sports is the most boring to watch on T.V.?**

Golf

51.4%

Soccer

17.1%

Bowling

17.1%

Tennis

8.6%

Baseball

5.7%

Responses: 105

☒ **What is your favorite sport?**

Football

32.4%

☑ **FAV**

Baseball

16.2%

I don't have a favorite

14.9%

Soccer

6.8%

Basketball

4.1%

Golf

2.7%

Volleyball

1.4%

Other

21.6%

Responses: 74

☒What is your favorite brand of athletic apparel?
-Poll Date: 28-Nov-2003

Nike

☑**FAV**

39.2%

Reebok

9.8%

Adidas

9.8%

Other

41.2%

Responses: 51

☒How should college football decide its post season?
-Poll Date: 11-Dec-2003

Playoff system

84.7%

Keep the BCS

8.3%

New ranking system

6.9%

Responses: 72

☒Who dominated his sport the most?

Michael Jordan

52.1%

Babe Ruth

22.3%

Wayne Gretzki

22.3%

Joe Montana

2.1%

Mike Tyson

1.1%

Responses: 94

☒Which college football team would win a match up between USC and LSU?
-Poll Date: 15-Jan-2004

USC

29.6%

LSU

18.4%

I'm not sure

4.1%

I don't really care

48.0%

Responses: 98

☑**CUR**

☒Who do you think will win the Super Bowl?
-Poll Date: 31-Jan-2004

New England Patriots

45.7%

Carolina Panthers

24.3%

I have no idea

30.0%

Responses: 70

☑**CUR**

☒Are referees biased?

Most of the time, yes

8.6%

Sometimes, yes

63.0%

Rarely

25.9%

Never

2.5%

Responses: 81

☑**CON**

Technology

☒ What is the greatest medium of communication?

Internet

40.8%

Television

31.2%

Phone

25.6%

Other

2.4%

Responses: 125

☒ Should spam be outlawed?

Yes

76.2%

No

15.1%

I'm not sure

8.7%

Responses: 126

☒ How old is your computer?

Less than one year old

21.4%

1–2 years old

28.6%

2–3 years old

28.6%

4–5 years old

17.9%

More than five years old

☐   3.6%

Responses: 112

☒Which modern invention would be most difficult to live without?

Telephone

▭   37.5%

Laundry machine

▭   30.0%

Computer

▭   15.0%

Television

▭   15.0%

Dishwasher

☐   2.5%

Responses: 80

☒Do you have a digital camera?

-Poll Date: 21-Jul-2003

Yes

▭   42.9%

No, but I plan on purchasing one

▭   20.0%

No, I have a film camera

▭   25.7%

I don't have a camera

☐   11.4%

Responses: 105

☒Has your computer ever been infected by a virus?

Yes

▭   51.9%

No

▭   48.1%

Responses: 106

☒**Would you support the creation of a do-not-spam registry?**

Yes

92.9%

No

3.1%

I'm not sure

4.1%

Responses: 98

☒**How would you describe your proficiency with the computer?**

Advanced

35.9%

Intermediate

52.4%

Novice

11.7%

Responses: 103

☒**Which of these is your favorite modern convenience?**

Computer

39.0%

☑**FAV**

Car

37.1%

Television

15.2%

Telephone

5.7%

Radio

2.9%

Responses: 105

☒**What is the best brand of computer?**

-Poll Date: 29-Dec-2003

Dell

37.5%

HP/Compaq

☐ 18.8%

Gateway

☐ 16.3%

IBM

☐ 5.0%

Sony

☐ 2.5%

NEC

☐ 1.3%

Micron

☐ 1.3%

Other

☐ 17.5%

Responses: 80

War of the Sexes

☒ **Who should be responsible for cooking meals at home?**

Mom
▭ 18.3%

Dad
▪ 0.0%

Both
▭▭▭▭ 81.7%

Responses: 153

☑**CON**

☒ **Is it acceptable for a man to be a stay-at-home parent while the wife works?**

Yes
▭▭▭▭ 90.4%

No
▪ 7.7%

I'm not sure
▪ 1.9%

Responses: 156

☑**CON**

☒ **In what sport are women better than men?**

Gymnastics
▭▭▭ 60.3%

Volleyball
▪ 9.6%

Swimming
▪ 4.1%

Track
▪ 2.7%

Soccer
▪ 0.7%

☑**CON**

None of the above

| | 22.6%

Responses: 146

☒What is the best solution to the toilet seat controversy?

Leave it down all the time

| | 48.8%   ☑**CON**

Before using the bathroom, females put the seat down/males put the seat up

| | 18.1%

After using the bathroom, females put the seat up/males put the seat down

☐ 7.1%

Leave it up all the time

☐ 3.1%

It doesn't really matter

| | 22.8%

Responses: 127

☒Are men and women equal?

Yes

| | 44.4%   ☑**CON**

No

| | 54.4%

I'm not sure

☐ 1.1%

Responses: 90

☒Should women be allowed to play in a PGA tournament?

Yes, if they can make the cut

| | 57.0%   ☑**CON**

I don't see a problem with it

| | 12.4%

No, the PGA is for men

| | 30.6%

Responses: 121

☒Who should be the one to pay on a date?

Whoever asked for the date

☑CON

| | 59.8% |

The man

| | 29.9% |

They should each pay for themselves

| | 9.3% |

The woman

| | 0.9% |

Responses: 107

☒Who would you rather have serve you at a restaurant?

Waiter

| | 9.2% |

Waitress

| | 25.0% |

Either one

| | 65.8% |

Responses: 76

☒Are women more caring than men?

Yes

☑CON

| | 67.9% |

No

| | 20.8% |

I'm not sure

| | 11.3% |

Responses: 106

☒Who should have the primary responsibility of raising children?

The man

☑CON

| | 0.0% |

The woman

| | 7.1% |

Both should share the responsibility equally

92.9%

Responses: 113

☒Are women less qualified than men to raise sons?

Yes

10.9%

☑CON

No

84.8%

I'm not sure

4.3%

Responses: 92

☒If you could trade places with someone from the opposite sex for a day, would you do it?

I'm male and I say yes

52.8%

☑HYP

I'm male and I say no

47.2%

Male Responses: 53

I'm female and I say yes

63.6%

I'm female and I say no

36.4%

Female Responses: 55

☒Which sex has more influence over the other?

I'm male and I say males do

22.6%

I'm male and I say females do

77.4%

Male Responses: 53

I'm female and I say males do

39.2%

I'm female and I say females do

[bar] 60.8%

Female Responses: 51

☒Do women receive less favorable treatment in the workplace compared to men?

I'm male and I say yes

[bar] 34.2%   ☑CON

I'm male and I say no

[bar] 65.8%

Male Responses: 38

I'm female and I say yes

[bar] 68.0%

I'm female and I say no

[bar] 32.0%

Female Responses: 50

☒Are women more wholesome than men?

I'm male and I say yes

[bar] 45.0%   ☑CON

I'm male and I say no

[bar] 55.0%

Male Responses: 40

I'm female and I say yes

[bar] 70.9%

I'm female and I say no

[bar] 29.1%

Female Responses: 55

☒If you were going to have a baby and could choose its gender, what would it be?

I'm male and I would choose a male

[bar] 58.3%

I'm male and I would choose a female

> 41.7%

Male Responses: 36

I'm female and I would choose a male

> 55.6%

I'm female and I would choose a female

> 44.4%

Female Responses: 54

☒Are men better leaders than women?

I'm male and I say yes

> 74.4%

I'm male and I say no

> 25.6%

Male Responses: 43

I'm female and I say yes

> 25.9%

I'm female and I say no

> 74.1%

Female Responses: 58

☑CON

War on Terror

☒**What do you think about the recent coverage of the 9-11 attacks?**
-Poll Date: 10-Sep-2002

It's great, keep it coming
| | 15.8%

I'm indifferent
| | 14.0%

It's making me depressed
| | 21.1%

Enough is enough already!
| | 49.1%

Responses: 57

☑CUR

☒**What do you think the status of Osama Bin Laden is?**
-Poll Date: 11-Sep-2002

Dead
| | 34.4%

Alive
| | 65.6%

Responses: 64

☑CUR

☒**Should we go to war with Iraq?**
-Poll Date: 08-Oct-2002

Yes
| | 47.6%

No
| | 40.5%

I'm not sure
| | 11.9%

Responses: 84

☑CUR

☑CON

☒ **Does the threat of terrorism justify limiting people's rights?**
-Poll Date: 11-Oct-2002

Yes
| 46.9%

No
| 53.1%

Responses: 81

☑**CUR**

☑**CON**

☒ **When will the next major terrorist attack occur in the U.S.?**
-Poll Date: 02-Dec-2002

Within the next six months
| 20.5%

Within the next year
| 37.6%

Within the next five years
| 17.1%

Within the next ten years
| 6.8%

There will not be another major terrorist attack on U.S. soil
| 17.9%

Responses: 117

☑**FUT**

☒ **Has the U.S. provided sufficient evidence to justify war with Iraq?**
-Poll Date: 28-Jan-2003

Yes
| 28.2%

No
| 59.2%

I'm not sure
| 12.7%

Responses: 142

☑**CUR**

☑**CON**

☒ **Is Saddam Hussein hiding weapons of mass destruction?**
-Poll Date: 11-Feb-2003

Yes
| 81.6%

☑**CUR**

No
☐   6.4%
I'm not sure
☐   12.1%
Responses: 141

☒If the U.S. does go to war with Iraq, how long will it last?
-Poll Date: 16-Feb-2003

A week or two
☐   11.9%   ☑CUR

A month or two
▭   33.3%   ☑FUT

Longer
▭   54.8%

Responses: 84

☒If Iraq used chemical/biological weapons against U.S. forces, should they respond with a nuclear weapon?
-Poll Date: 04-Mar-2003

Yes, only if there were an extreme amount of U.S. casualties
▭   24.8%   ☑CUR

Yes, in any case
▭   22.0%   ☑HYP

No
▭   46.1%

I'm not sure
☐   7.1%

Responses: 141

☒Will the world be better off or worse off if the U.S. goes to war with Iraq?
-Poll Date: 12-Mar-2003

Better off
▭   40.6%   ☑CUR

Worse off
▭   31.3%   ☑CON

I'm not sure

28.1%

Responses: 128

☒Do you think Saddam Hussein will attempt to use biological/chemical weapons against the U.S. and it's allies?
-Poll Date: 19-Mar-2003

Yes

75.2%

☑**CUR**

No

8.8%

I'm not sure

16.1%

Responses: 137

☒How is the war against Iraq proceeding?
-Poll Date: 21-Mar-2003

Better than I expected

38.5%

☑**CUR**

About how I expected

57.7%

Worse than I expected

3.8%

Responses: 104

☒Do you think Saddam Hussein is dead?
-Poll Date: 22-Mar-2003

Yes

12.8%

☑**CUR**

No

61.7%

I'm not sure

25.5%

Responses: 94

☒ Do you support the troops fighting in Iraq?
-Poll Date: 26-Mar-2003

Yes

☑ **CUR**

[████████████████] 72.4%

Yes, but I'm against the war

[████] 23.6%

No

[▢] 2.4%

I'm indifferent

[▢] 1.6%

Responses: 123

☒ Would Iraq fire a missile at its own civilians so it could blame it on the U.S.?
-Poll Date: 29-Mar-2003

Yes

☑ **CUR**

[██████████████████] 87.1%

☑ **HYP**

No

[▢] 4.3%

I'm not sure

[▢] 8.6%

Responses: 93

☒ Is the U.S. winning the public relations war with Iraq?
-Poll Date: 01-Apr-2003

Yes

☑ **CUR**

[████] 30.6%

No

[██████] 42.5%

I'm not sure

[████] 26.9%

Responses: 134

☒ What is the primary reason the coalition is at war with Iraq?
-Poll Date: 07-Apr-2003

To remove Saddam Hussein from power

☑ **CUR**

[██████] 41.4%

To rid Iraq of weapons of mass destruction

☐ 16.4%

To secure Iraq's oil

☐ 13.6%

To gain a strategic military presence in the Middle East

☐ 11.4%

To liberate the Iraqi people

☐ 9.3%

Other

☐ 7.9%

Responses: 140

☒ Should France and Germany play a role in the reconstruction of Iraq?

-Poll Date: 12-Apr-2003

Yes, they should play a major role

☐ 16.1%

Yes, they should play a minor role

☐ 30.1%

No

☐ 48.4%

I'm not sure

☐ 5.4%

Responses: 93

☑ CUR

☑ CON

☒ Was it the right decision to go to war with Iraq?

-Poll Date: 03-Jun-2003

Yes

☐ 59.7%

No

☐ 23.3%

I'm not sure

☐ 17.1%

Responses: 129

☑ CUR

☑ CON

☒Should Saddam Hussein be caught dead or alive?

-Poll Date: 04-Aug-2003

Dead

☐ 24.3%

Alive

☐ 15.9%

Either way

☐ 59.8%

Responses: 107

☑CUR

☒Are you in favor of the United State's method of using pre-emptive attacks to combat terrorism?

Yes

☐ 45.0%

No

☐ 28.0%

I'm not sure

☐ 27.0%

Responses: 100

☑CON

☒Should the U.S. pull out of Iraq?

-Poll Date: 01-Nov-2003

Yes

☐ 46.9%

No

☐ 37.5%

I'm not sure

☐ 15.6%

Responses: 32

☑CUR

☒How do you view Saudi Arabia in relation to the U.S.?

Untrustworthy

☐ 63.9%

Terrorist nation

☐ 18.0%

☑CON

Neutral

☐   13.1%

True ally

☐   4.9%

Responses: 61

☒ Should countries that opposed the war on Iraq be allowed to bid on reconstruction contracts?

-Poll Date: 12-Dec-2003

Yes

☐   23.7%   ☑ **CUR**

No

☐   71.0%   ☑ **CON**

I'm not sure

☐   5.4%

Responses: 93

☒ What is the relationship between Islam and terrorism?

There is an unusually high amount of terrorists practicing Islam   ☑ **CON**

☐   43.4%

A few bad apples spoil the bunch

☐   30.2%

Islam promotes terrorist ideals

☐   15.1%

There are no more Islamic terrorists than in any other religion

☐   7.5%

It's merely a coincidental relationship

☐   3.8%

Responses: 53

Work

☒ **How do you like your job?**

I love my job!
[bar] 20.0%

I'm content
[bar] 26.0%

It's okay
[bar] 16.3%

It's not that great
[bar] 11.2%

I hate my job!
[bar] 5.1%

I don't have a job right now
[bar] 21.4%

Responses: 215

☒ **What would happen if a principal wage earner in you house was laid-off?**

Bankruptcy
[bar] 20.0%

Would have to sell assets to make ends meet
[bar] 22.5%

Just barely be able to make it
[bar] 24.2%

Make some cuts but otherwise be okay
[bar] 27.5%

Still live comfortably
[bar] 5.8%

Responses: 120

☒ Have you ever wanted to join the military?

Yes
☐ 30.1%

No
☐ 57.1%

I was in the military
☐ 11.3%

I am in the military
☐ 1.5%

Responses: 133

☒ How do you get to work?

Bus
☐ 3.9%

Drive alone
☐ 78.7%

Car pool
☐ 5.5%

Walk
☐ 4.7%

Other
☐ 7.1%

Responses: 127

☒ Which would be the least desirable low-wage job?

Dishwasher
☐ 38.2%

Janitor
☐ 22.4%

Fast food cook
☐ 22.4%

Farm hand
☐ 9.2%

Box boy
☐ 7.9%

Responses: 76

☒ Have you ever been fired from a job?

Yes
☐ 38.5%

No
☐ 61.5%

Responses: 104

☒ How much overtime do you work?

1 to 5 hours a week
☐ 22.3%

6 to 10 hours a week
☐ 6.4%

11 to 15 hours a week
☐ 8.5%

More than 15 hours a week
☐ 3.2%

I rarely work overtime
☐ 23.4%

I never work overtime
☐ 36.2%

Responses: 94

☒ Is outsourcing jobs to foreign countries un-American?
-Poll Date: 11-Aug-2003

Yes
☐ 47.0%

No
☐ 37.3%

I'm not sure
☐ 15.7%

Responses: 83

☑CUR

☑CON

☒How have you been affected by layoffs?

-Poll Date: 07-Jan-2004

I haven't been affected

| 56.7%

Someone close to me has been laid-off

| 28.9%

I have been laid-off

| 14.4%

Responses: 90

☑CUR

World

☒ **Should America force North Korea to dismantle its nuclear weapons?**
-Poll Date: 21-Oct-2002

Yes
☑**CUR**

62.3%

No

21.9%

I'm not sure

15.8%

Responses: 456

☒ **What will be the next country to use a nuclear weapon?**

North Korea
☑**FUT**

23.0%

United States

18.3%

Pakistan

9.5%

China

6.3%

India

3.2%

Russia

0.8%

No one will

30.2%

Other

8.7%

Responses: 126

☒ **Do you think the United States will go to war with North Korea in the next 10 years?**
-Poll Date: 17-Feb-2003

Yes

☑**CUR**

43.4%

No

☑**FUT**

27.4%

I'm not sure

29.2%

Responses: 113

☒ **How do you feel about taking the "French" out of "French Fries"?**
-Poll Date: 15-Mar-2003

It's a great idea

☑**CUR**

23.7%

I'm indifferent

☑**COM**

16.5%

It's a dumb idea

59.8%

Responses: 97

☒ **How do you feel about the anti-American sentiment in Europe?**
-Poll Date: 05-Apr-2003

It's justified

☑**CUR**

11.3%

It's partly justified

40.0%

It's unjustified

45.0%

I'm not sure

3.8%

Responses: 80

☒Would tensions with Israel in the Middle East subside if the Palestinians had their own country?

-Poll Date: 21-May-2003

Yes

☑CUR

33.3%

No

☑CON

45.6%

I'm not sure

21.1%

Responses: 114

☒What side do you support in the Israel/Palestine conflict?

-Poll Date: 14-Nov-2003

Israel

☑CUR

44.9%

Palestine

5.6%

Neither, they are equally at fault

49.4%

Responses: 89

☒Why do Middle Eastern citizens hate America?

The influence of their leaders

32.6%

Because America is a non-Muslim country

29.2%

American foreign policy

28.1%

The influence of their media

5.6%

Because American troops are based there

4.5%

Responses: 89

☒Who would be number one on a top ten list of the world's most wicked leaders?

Adolf Hitler

☐ 69.3%

Joseph Stalin

☐ 14.9%

Osama bin Laden

☐ 8.9%

Saddam Hussein

☐ 2.0%

Slobodan Milosevic

☐ 0.0%

Other

☐ 2.0%

I'm not sure

☐ 3.0%

Responses: 101

Attraction Survey

Survey respondents were asked to rank the factors that attract them to the opposite sex. Respondents listed the top ten overall attraction factors, the top three facial factors, and the top three body factors.

The results are listed in order by using a point system. For overall factors, first place votes received ten points, second place nine, and so on. For body and facial factors, first place votes received three points, second place two, and third place one. Total points are listed with first place votes in parenthesis.

153 men and 151 women responded to the survey.

Women

⊠ **What overall factors attract you to the opposite sex?**

Personality
1288(81)

Face
852(22)

Intellect
802(10)

Mutual Interests
718(6)

Confidence
701(7)

Physique
499(7)

Height
467(5)

Clothes
426(0)

Family Relations
386(3)

Spirituality
378(8)

Voice
259(0)

Reputation
218(0)

Hair
210(0)

Earning Ability
189(0)

Muscles
174(0)

Athleticism
156(0)

Talent
☐   144(0)
Work Position
☐   105(0)
Cologne
☐   104(0)
Skin Tone
☐   92(0)
Money/Possessions
☐   77(1)
Popularity
☐   60(1)

☒What factors attract you to a man's face?

Eyes
☐────────────────────   382(95)
Smile
☐──────────────   277(38)
Lips
☐─────   126(11)
Facial Hair
☐   42(2)
Jaw
☐   40(3)
Nose
☐   28(1)
Cheeks
☐   11(1)

☒What factors attract you to a man's body?

Arms
☐────────   215(41)
Stomach
☐────   141(24)

Hands

138(24)

Butt

135(21)

Skin

134(23)

Chest

64(9)

Legs

51(5)

Neck

20(2)

Men

☒What overall factors attract you to the opposite sex?

Personality

1208(48)

Physique

1078(27)

Face

1045(38)

Intellect

738(8)

Mutual Interests

703(9)

Confidence

639(7)

Clothes

410(2)

Voice

323(1)

Hair

323(1)

Spirituality
☐ 272(5)

Skin Tone
☐ 267(3)

Height
☐ 235(0)

Family Relations
☐ 200(3)

Talent
☐ 196(0)

Athleticism
☐ 182(0)

Reputation
☐ 171(0)

Perfume
☐ 111(0)

Popularity
☐ 86(1)

Muscles
☐ 83(0)

Earning Ability
☐ 55(0)

Work Position
☐ 50(0)

Money/Possessions
☐ 40(0)

☒What factors attract you to a women's face?

Eyes
☐ 401(105)

Smile
☐ 269(38)

Lips
☐ 160(3)

Cheeks

☐   41(6)

Nose

☐   24(1)

Makeup

☐   10(0)

Jaw

☐   7(0)

☒ What factors attract you to a women's body?

Butt

☐ 276(58)

Breasts

☐ 251(41)

Legs

☐ 183(27)

Stomach

☐ 89(6)

Skin

☐ 67(12)

Neck

☐ 22(4)

Hands

☐ 16(3)

Arms

☐ 6(0)

Age Group Differences

This section was created to illustrate the gap between what younger and older generations find attractive. The following is a list of notable differences among two of the age groups surveyed: 25 and under, and 46 and above.

Notable differences among males:

Factor:	<=25—Rank:	>=46—Rank:	Difference:
Athleticism	12	20	8
Reputation	16	8	8
Clothes	7	14	7
Mutual Interests	6	2	4
Spirituality	11	7	4
Talent	15	11	4

Notable differences among females:

Factor:	<=25—Rank:	>=46—Rank:	Difference:
Voice	11	5	6
Money/Possessions	22	16	6
Physique	6	10	4
Height	8	12	4
Muscles	13	17	4
Talent	17	13	4

Afterword

I hope you enjoyed reading this book and, in small part, gained a new perspective on what others think and do.

If you have any comments, suggestions, or ideas for future polls, I would love to hear from you!

Please contact me at: areyouthinking@att.net.

0-595-32797-4